Millie McCall's Full Moon Poker Night

Sara Williams

Millie McCall's

Full Moon Poker Night

A novella and tales from the San Juan Islands

by

Sara Williams

publisher@cayouvalley.com

First Edition: Feb. 2014

Cover Design by Ginna Magee

Author Photograph by Anne Remington

Interior Design and Production by Colin & Winston Williams

ACKNOWLEDGMENTS

South Carolina author and book reviewer Douglas Quinn prompted me to write a fictional version of an Orcas Island tale. Doug needed several a poker-themed novellas to round out his anthology, *Four of a Kind*, which was published by White Heron Press in 2012.

Meanwhile, the San Juan Islands I've called home for thirty years were named a National Monument, and so it occurred to me that some readers might enjoy stories about the island culture, where it is said that one must be a card-carrying character just count as an island dweller. At that point, I decided to republish Millie McCall together with some tales from these islands, plus a few from the rural communities of the Pacific Northwest.

My version of the building of Rosario, home of former Seattle mayor Robert Moran, was inspired by conclusions I drew from an historical account written by Rosario manager and musician Christopher Peacock.

A few islanders are named outright in these tales. They are the winners of naming rights auctions to benefit our magnificent performing arts hall, the Orcas Center. For their support and inspiration I would like to thank Gail Glasser, who named the mysterious poker dealer in "Millie" for her mother, and wanted her dressed in gowns by her friend Victor Costa. Avid motorcycle riders and card players Duff and Marilyn Andrews would definitely have been invited to one of Millie's poker nights, and Eska Wilson's exotic first name was a perfect archetype for the wise mother in "The Time I was Road Kill."

My thanks to My good friend Dan Byers, a character in his own right from the historic town of Goldendale in the southeastern corner of Washington State, a Realtor/raconteur who knows a good story to pass along when he hears one. Dan's a fellow who'll lend out a hand, a wrench, a truck or whatever. When in need of a last name for the lovely Lara in my Mountaindale wedding story, I borrowed Dan's last name.

I am forever indebted to Sally and Larry Cornelius of Goldendale for their years of generous hospitality and support..

Florida author and expert poker player Ben Shelfer vetted my scandalous poker game.

CONTENTS

For my beloved husband Bill whose hilarious tales of life at the Buckhorn Lodge served as an inspiration for this book.

MILLIE MCCALL'S
FULL MOON POKER NIGHT

The tide was out and the dock rode high overhead. I shut off the outboard and let my boat drift toward the pilings. Above me, I could see a pair of brown legs scissoring toward me in short shorts as Carla Bridges rushed to lend a hand. She waved for the bow line and I swung it long and wide, so as not to smack her upside the head. She caught my line and hanked it around a cleat.

I hoisted a dripping ling cod over one shoulder of my rain slicker, slung a ditty bag over the other, and one-handed my way up the dock ladder, stepping carefully onto planking slick with the morning dew. "Ding a ling, Carla. Fresh ling for dinner, straight out of Ben's favorite cod hole."

Carla smiled, but it wasn't her full-on smile. As her long, doleful face emerged from wisps of fog, I could see that her eyes were red, her lips were blue, and her deep tan had gone a greenish yellow. I dropped the cod at her feet and swept her into my arms. She's a big woman, a gawky woman, and I liked the size of her, seeing as how I'd turned eighteen and grown as tall as I ever hoped to be, six four, a two inch advantage over John J. Halprin, my formidable dad, not to mention a head taller than Carla's husband, Ben.

"You look wrecked, Carla—beautiful but wrecked."

Carla managed an ironic version of her usual sensual laugh. From the growl of it I just knew that Ben was trying Carla's patience again. "I thought Ben was dead, Jim, I really did. He scared the life right out of me this time."

I turned my face away, hiding my smile. Ben Bridges was a handful, no doubt about it. There was a streak of the wild child in him, which is what I loved about the man.

Ben Bridges hunted. He fished. He dived. He sailed. Ben Bridges made a career out of sport. He rendered rocks and trees into cash. It was Ben's independent spirit that my own dad envied; it was amazing to me to see how my father, a wealthy druggist with a chain of stores, a respected state legislator, and a national grand orator of the Masonic lodge, it was amazing how John J. Halprin loved nothing more than to escape here to the San Juan Islands and hang out with Ben.

The best thing of all, what made me ecstatic, was when we headed out to sea in Ben's Owens 44. Once we were clear of the local channels, Dad and Ben would get into a poker game and leave me to steer the boat, The Nightcap, she was, and what a beauty. A more cautious skipper would never have let a green kid take the helm of such a vessel, but that was Ben. He took risks, and sometimes things went wrong, which was why Carla had summoned me from my summer job on Sucia Island.

"I got your message, Carla. Tell me what happened."

"I'll let the Great Man tell you himself," Carla snarled. "I have about three minutes to get the breakfast going for twenty five guests and I never could light that beast of a stove."

"I'll do it, Carla," I said in my bitty kid voice, making Carla laugh. We both laughed until our eyes were wet at how I'd burned my fingers and singed my eyebrows as an eight-year-old kid trying to light the enormous propane stove in the Bridges' BakerVue Lodge on the north shore of Orcas Island. I was determined to prove myself to Ben or blow through the roof trying.

The year I turned eight, the mid 70s this was, I'd celebrated my birthday at the lodge. When our family's month was over and our entire tribe was to be bundled back to Olympia prior to the opening of the legislative session, I begged Ben and Carla to let me stay on for the rest of the season. I swore to my parents I'd earn straight A's when school began. I'd chop kindling and catch fish and fill the gas tanks of the arriving boaters. I promised Carla I'd help clean cabins and fold laundry, and so it was for a few glorious weeks I escaped the formal routines of my mother's household where I ranked a lowly and lost number ten in a family of eleven. I had nine older sisters and a baby brother. As the first male heir, I was coddled and spoiled, when what I yearned to be was a man, a Ben Bridges style man. Ben had the respect of my formidable dad.

2

I followed Carla into the lodge where I plopped my glorious catch into a cooler and iced the fish, a ling cod that would feed the house for dinner. Carla cringed as I waved a lighted match over the hissing pilot light of the massive stove, resulting in an impressive pop and a blue blast. Carla thanked me as she tied on her chef's apron and shooed me out of the kitchen. I told her I'd look in on Ben.

"He's in bed," Carla said. "If he's asleep, please don't wake him. If he's awake, try not to cringe when you see him."

Ben never could stop building onto things; his newest edition to the lodge was a master wing, a long stroll down a hall from the great room. "Mr. Ben?" I said softly, rapping on the handsome red fir doorframe.

"Jim Boy." Ben sputtered out my name with as much gusto as he could muster; a fit of coughing followed, a wet hacking cough, and when that subsided he raised his head enough that I offered him a sip of water through a straw. He motioned me to sit in the faded velvet wing chair beside the fireplace, but first I stoked the fire to a roar the way Ben had taught me to do. "I've busted a rib or two and it hurts like hell to laugh," Ben croaked, "so go easy with the light bulb jokes."

The shades were drawn in the room but even in the dim firelight it pained me to look at the man. He was one long bruise from scalp to waist. Raw red patches were torn in his thick salt and pepper hair. A ragged cut in his cheek had been closed with stitches that would never pass muster on one of my mother's quilts. Both hands were heavily bandaged and his speech was slurred on account of his jaw had been wired shut.

"It looks to me the joke's on you, Ben," I said. "What was it? Ten rounds with a grizzly?"

"I was trying to do my own cat skinning, damn fool that I am."

"Tell me about it."

"Later," he mumbled. "Too hard to talk. My lips are blubber; my throat's pure sawdust. Carla must have poisoned me on some dope."

"Yeah, right, Ben. So maybe you should try taking your medicine the way the doctor ordered." I turned out the light. "I'll fill in for you in the dining room while you rest."

"There's one more thing I need you to do, Jim. I've gotten myself into a sticky situation and I need you to get me out of it."

That's how I found myself accepting an invitation to Millie

McCall's full moon poker party. I presented myself late that very same Saturday evening in the drawing room of the Lookout Inn, an old railroad wayside of a place with a fine view of Eastsound. The Lookout had fallen into disrepair and was now open for business, the project of a very ambitious pair of newcomers who were viewed with deep suspicion by most of the islanders, but befriended by Ben.

Two other players were already there, seated on one of those circular sofas you'd see in Victorian era hotel lobbies. This pair stared at me apprehensively, me in my biker boots and my leathers, way ragged and underdressed compared to them.

They had their backs to the formal portrait of Olympia, the nude with the black ribbon round her neck, lounging in bed with a faraway look on her face. I'd managed to stay awake through enough of my art history classes to realize that this portrait, with the Olympic mountain range painted into the background, was a Cascade country knockoff of the famous painting by the French Impressionist Édouard Manet. In this updated version of Olympia, the lady is more voluptuous, wears more strategic drapery, and the orange flowers that seem to grow from the side of her head are a bunch of the orange tiger lilies that grow in abundance here on the Island. Of course the church ladies, not being art history types, were scandalized by Olympia.

A squat and swarthy fellow dressed in a ruffled, Pepto Bismal pink evening shirt rose and shook my hand. Seeing as how he wore a black eyepatch, he resembled an overweight and battered flamingo. I shook his extended hand.

"Bob Hamer," he said, "Bob's Electric? I did the rewire on the BakerVue for Ben. Back there his first season? When the county shut him down? Weren't you the kid who hung around the lodge?"

"Jim Halprin. I adopted Ben as my alter-dad when I was eight years old. Best move I ever made. I'm standing in for Ben. He sends his regrets."

"I heard there was some sort of accident?"

"Typical Ben. Out to save himself a bundle on his new development by putting in his own roads. Bought himself a worn out old Cat with the tread falling off. Carla told me Ben put in weeks out there gouging a road out of the mountainside north of the lodge."

"Raccoon Point?"

"Right. He'd roughed in a few miles of road, to where the cliffs .

are just about vertical. Fortunately, Carla went out in the Jeep to take him his lunch. She felt this tremor and saw it all, the road collapsed under him; the cliff above him gave way, burying Ben, tractor and all, right up to his neck."

"Carla had Ben right where she wanted him for once," said the other guy, a handsome blond dude in a Mexican style denim jacket with dragons embroidered on it.

"You've got that right," I said, shaking his hand.

"Larry Fenton," he said. "I volunteer with the fire department? I answered the aid call. It took seven of us the better part of three hours to dig Ben out. He's lucky to be alive."

"Ben'll be first to agree with you—found out he's no Cat skinner," I said. "And then he tells me he needs me to show up here tonight in my Harley-style tuxedo so's not to ruin Mrs. McCall's poker party."

Fenton and Hamer gave me the once over, me in biker garb with my braid dripping down my back, and my Fu Manchu moustache. The pair of them laughed out loud and clapped me on the back and said I was in for a time. They told me that Mrs. McCall would be here any minute now and refused to say anything more—wouldn't want to spoil a guy's fun. "So what are we playing?"

"Texas Hold'Em," Hamer said.

"Hold'Em until midnight," Fenton murmured, "After midnight it's All Holds Barred."

"Uh oh," I said. "Not double or nothing, I hope?" I fingered the wad of cash Ben had shoved at me. He told me if I did good before midnight I was to cash out and make a run for it. Ben was an amazing card player, and he schooled me in poker when he didn't have me chopping wood. We'd play for pennies. He'd front me a dollar and if I lost it, I was out. The only way to stay alive as a poker player was to limit your loss before the first hand was dealt, and to cash in your chips while you still had some. In this case, a week's proceeds from the BakerVue was what Ben could spare. Lose more than that and Carla would declare a pox on both of us, and a pox applied by Carla Bridges was at least eight turns of the screw on the way down to the fiery lake.

"Double or nothing?" Fenton said, raising his golden eyebrows, thick enough to comb. Fenton was this Adonis of a dude with pale grey eyes and a square chin. "What do you say, Bob?"

"I'd say not for nothing's more like it."

"This Millie McCall," I said, "We are talking *the* McCalls? The McCall fortune, right? Ted McCall bought the old Rosario property and built a mansion. Foxglove, he calls it. Do I have my facts straight?"

Bob chopped me off with a back-handed swat followed by a forefinger raised to his pursed lips: "Listen." He squinted, making a show of checking his watch. "A punctual woman, right on time as usual."

"So? I don't see…"

Outside the Inn I heard that sweet, deep rumbling of the pipes so dear to me. "A *Harley?* Mrs. McCall rides a *Harley?*" My remark sent Hamer and Fenton into peals of laughter that they quickly suppressed as we heard the rushed voice of the Lookout Inn's managing partner Todd Fircloth barking orders. The glass doors of the lobby swung open and Todd's baritone, sliding along with a trombone's grace, delivered his nth degree of gush: "Millie, dearest. We are sooooo delighted to see you once again."

Millie's voice had a gargly quality as she flirted right back. "Todd, darling. How is the Island's most eligible male?"

"I'm available, Millie, but you, my love, are taken…"

Behind closed doors, Fenton's mouth turned down, his eyes bugged and he shook his head as he pantomimed Fircloth's syrupy tones. The doors to the drawing room swung open, and Larry was caught with his hand on his heart and his mouth open; Bob Hamer swiped tears out of his good eye and wiped them on the ruffled cuff of his screaming pink shirt.

"Well now, look who we have here," Mrs. McCall said, "Larrrr-y Fenton, the golden boy of the Island firefighters. Look at you. I must arrange to send you down to Hollywood for a screen test."

I stared, my mouth hanging open, as Mrs. McCall clumped across the room and into Fenton's arms, her gait defined by the clunky Doc Marten boots laced the length of her shins. She was a strong-looking woman, broad shouldered. She lurched along with a certain biker's swagger, but the moves didn't quite jibe with her lost, little girl features and the snarl of sun-bleached brown hair that fell to her shoulders. The flaming red gown she wore swirled around her knees, a nightgown I swear--a flimsy sort of negligee, a too-revealing thing I'd see my sisters loll around the house in when my mother wasn't home to catch them at it.

Avoiding outright scandal, Millie wore a Harley leather jacket over her nightgown. The jacket was a custom job with strings of leather fringe tipped in conchos, those Mexican style silver do-dads that cowboys wore on their chaps, adopted by us Harley-style cowpokes. Millie wore the jacket draped around her shoulders like a stole. Her biker helmet hung over her arm by the strap, handbag-style. I gaped at her, admiring the succulence of her white skin. Millie McCall was as pale as a mushroom in the moonlight.

Millie turned to Bob Hamer who had by this time regained his composure, and sucked in his belly.

"Bob, darling, you must come to the McCall Company Oscar party. We need you to show those silly peacocks who pass themselves off as actors how a real man wears a shirt."

Millie planted a kiss on Bob's cheek, his face turning as pink as his shirt as she raved about his amazing taste. She gave his arm a squeeze. Bob looked as if he wanted to kiss the place where she had touched him and then it was my turn.

As she stared up at me, I gaped right back. Millie McCall was a freaking mess. Her sort of grooming would never have passed muster in my household where ten women primping around the clock meant that finding a couple of minutes in one of our five bathrooms was no easy task.

Miz McCall's hair, black at the roots, hadn't met a comb in the last twenty four hours, or was it thirty six? A thick smear of red lipstick overran the borders of her babe-style mouth. A false eyelid that had come unglued was stuck to the top of her right eye socket. Her kewpie doll blue eyes peered out from beneath Brillo brows that needed mowing. Rings of yesterday's mascara underscored the puffiness around her eyes. By some trick of nature, however, Millie McCall's dishevelment underscored her waif-style beauty. She had that wasted look that later became a fashion statement in snooty magazines.

Millie had one of those lost child/woman faces that we Americans are wild for, the Doris Day type, the Marilyn Monroe child, the Judy Garland pixie face, the big eyes, the short chin, the perky nose, combined with an attitude of weariness, of grief. There was that quality about Mrs. McCall as she fixed me with her electric blue stare; I read desperation, vulnerability, and maybe a touch of madness in her expression. The hackles on the back of my neck stood up and saluted. Millie McCall struck me as the sort of siren my mother and my sisters deplored, the sort who could seduce a guy in one minute and cry rape the next. No wonder Ben Bridges had warned me to run at the first opportunity.

"Well what have we here?" Her thick tongue flicked over her lips as she extended her hand, moving in close as she did so, giving me the come hither out of the corner of her eyes. Up close I could tell she was t least ten years older than I was, which, of course, made her even more alluring.

"I'm Millie McCall."

"Pleased to meet you Mrs. McCall," I was careful to keep my eyes pinned to her face and not to let them snag in the ample cleavage nesting in the leathery fringe of her motorcycle jacket. "Jim Halprin, standing in for Ben Bridges. He sends his regrets."

"Is something wrong?" Tone petulant, mouth pouty; I noticed what I'd missed before: Millie had an involuntary tic. A pull of her mouth and a twitch of an eye punctuated every third or fourth sentence.

"Ben had a run-in with the side of a mountain."

The dark eyes widened. Her hand found mine. Her icy fingers squeezed my damp, hot hand. "I heard something about an avalanche. I'm so sorry. I had no idea Ben was involved."

"He'll pull through. Ben is one rugged guy."

"Yes, he does have quite a reputation. I'll have to pay him a visit-- such a nice man. I met him on the ferry, but I haven't yet met his wife."

"Carla Bridges will be delighted to meet you, Mrs. McCall." *Carla will be thrilled to have some heiress/hussy come calling on her husband in her nightgown.*

"Call me Millie, won't you, Jim? Otherwise we won't be friends. That would be tragic since we are both ardent bikers. I assume that Fat Boy softail out there belongs to you?"

"Yes, ma'am."

Her eyes raked me over, from the braid to the boots. "A Fat Boy for a big boy. It fits."

"I have to say, it gives me some room." I flexed my arms out full length, measuring the distance to the handlebars, and straightened my back in the ramrod posture that the burly machine configured on its rider. My leather jacket made the appropriate creaks. "I started out on a low rider, but got into one too many high centers on a logging road." The real truth was, I had totaled Ben Bridges' old shovelhead is what I did. Ben bought us a Fat Boy, one of the new models with the Vs engine, and I earned my part of the co-ownership by doing all the cleaning and the maintenance under Ben's demanding eye, a deal that my dad didn't exactly approve of, but he never could say no to Ben.

"Low riders were never meant for off road," she said.

"Yes Ma'am."

"Yes Millie." She turned to the other two fellows, who chimed in with 'Yes Millie.' A waiter rolled in a serving cart loaded with tiny crab cakes, oysters on the half shell and spicy meatballs and, ravenous dude that I was back then, I devoured more than my share of the appetizers.

Whiskey was offered, which I had the good sense to decline, following the cue of Eyepatch Bob, who stuck to ginger ale. Millie had one glass of champagne, that was it, and so I ruled out alcohol being responsible for the odd gleam in her eye. Larry took his whiskey neat and poured it down as if it were soda pop and had another, whereupon a less diffident side of his nature emerged and it was Larry Fenton who pried Millie away from me and installed her at the table where the play began.

"Only one table? I thought this was a tournament," I remarked to Fircloth as he passed my chair.

Todd smirked. "Millie likes her games to be intimate." Fircloth had provided an exquisitely polished, marquetry inlaid table for the occasion. Five places were set, and I had assumed that Todd himself would sit in as dealer. Millie asked me to serve as the blind and present the formal bid. The stakes were low, set at five and ten dollars, much to my relief.

Once we were all seated, the eyes of the other players followed Fircloth as he swept through the doorway with a stately redhead on his arm. She was dressed in what amounted to a floor-length black satin slip held up with black spaghettis straps, the thinnest of vermicelli, if you get what I mean. The swishy black fabric clung to every curve as she moved with the predatory stroll of a runway veteran. Her center-parted hair was swept into a sculpted mound, topping her heart-shaped, wide-eyed face. She wore a black ribbon around her neck. A bright cluster of orange tiger lilies was pinned just above her left ear.

"May I present Miss Olympia, your dealer for the evening," Fircloth announced, poker-faced.

"Olympia," Millie said, "just lovely."

"I should say so." Larry Fenton applauded politely and we all joined in. "So nice to see you, for real. I always wondered how you would look in a dress." We all had a good laugh over Larry's wisecrack, and "Olympia," smiled ever so slightly.

Who was this vision? How had such a spectacular creature found her way to the Island? She was nearly as tall as I was, and if she had been on Orcas before, I would surely have noticed her. Was she a new counselor at one of the island's summer camps? If so, Todd Fircloth must have spirited her away from her minders for the night.

At this eccentric table, I had the good fortune to be seated to her left. Or maybe not so good. She wore a spicy perfume that intoxicated me. She smiled politely at every remark I made in an attempt to get her attention, as she dealt out the hands with the finesse of some Las Vegas dealer. I must admit I spent more time sneaking peaks at "Olympia" than I did studying the cards on the table: her straight, reddish brows, her limpid brown eyes, the dimple in her cheek, the graceful sweep of her straight nose, the roll of fullness beneath her pointed chin, and her glistening freshwater pearl earrings, nearly as orange as the cluster of tiger lilies that shimmered in her hair when she bent to ruffle the deck of Bicycles.

Unfortunately my frank admiration of Olympia gained me no traction whatever at the table. The first two cards she dealt me were symbolic but not so practical, a K-7, which Ben called a "king salmon," or a "Columbia river". The flop yielded Canadian aces and a sailboat —a pair of queens and a 4.

"Good gracious Miss Olympia," I muttered under my breath so that only she could hear. "What a flop this is—I am a flop." Her shoulders raised, her lips betrayed amusement, but nothing more. Olympia refused to look at me as I smooth-called after the other players raised. The turn yielded a luscious fat lady, the 8, and while I might be a fat admirer, I knew I was drawing dead. Larry Fenton and I mucked our cards as Millie and Eyepatch playfully raised each other.

When sweet Olympia dealt out the river card, it turned out to be a stinking crab, a 3, so that's where I would have fallen into the river and drowned. Eyepatch Bob raked in the pot with a pair of kings. I soon learned he was the player to beat since Millie and Goldenboy Fenton were too busy flirting with each other to pay attention to the game. Bob put his eyepatch to good use, turning it to the table. He kept his good eye hidden behind a squint and his body as still as a hunter in a blind, so I found him impossible to read. I had rags all night, terrible cards, monkey cards. I finally caught a wired pair of fishhooks, jacks, only to see Eyepatch Bob run them down, filling a gut-shot straight on the river. He was having a whale of a night.

Goldenboy Fenton teased him. "I've never seen you play so good, Bob. It has to be that pink shirt."

Millie wasn't doing well. She had a distracting habit of mumbling to herself. She stared at Olympia, shaking her head, sneaking peaks at her dress. "Valentino?" She muttered, shaking her head. "Victor Costa?" She bet heavily on every round, and seemed to relish shoving chips in Bob's direction. I couldn't figure her out. Was she mad at her husband and determined to throw his money around? Or was she put off by the fact that the luscious young dealer had aced her with her better dress?

We'd played for a couple of hours when Millie called for a break. She gathered her helmet and swaggered out into the hall. We heard the front door slam. I was relieved. The cards were running against me. What bets I had made were paltry. At least I'd hung on to the vast part of Ben's stake.

"Millie's going to be awhile," Bob said. "We're going out for air. Care to join us?" I yearned to stay behind and nip on the Courvoisier on the sideboard, hoping that Olympia would reappear so that I could score a word with her, but I was afraid I'd fall asleep from pure boredom and so I followed my buddies out the front door.

The Lookout Inn faces on a sound as deep as some Norwegian fiord. The tide was way out, the moon gleaming on a land bridge to a rocky atoll known as Indian Island, a few hundred yards in front of the Inn. Said land bridge appears now and then in the event of extremely low tide. Moonlight at this latitude turns the night white, rendering the sound as glassy as sleet on ice. It was easy to see a trail of footprints gashed in wet sand.

The footprints belonged to a slender figure standing on the atoll beside a snarl of tree branches bleached in the moonlight, her hands stretched upward, embracing the dazzling moon.

"Is that Millie out there?" I hoped I was not seeing what I believed I had.

"That's her," Bob said.

"What's she doing out there?"

"We don't ask," Larry said.

A half hour elapsed where Bob and Larry smoked, supplanting the mellow night air with its scents of sea salt and cedar with a thick cigarette stench. They headed inside perhaps to partake of the cognac. I stayed behind, watching for Millie McCall. As it happened, I had a distant connection with the founder of the McCall fortune, Cash McCall. There was a real Cash McCall, by the way, as opposed to the sleek dude played by James Garner in the movies. The real Cash, the pioneering Cash, made a killing outfitting miners in the Alaska gold rush, while my great, great Uncle Charles made it large as a grain broker in Spokane. Uncle Charles had done some land deals in the rich Palouse Country down in the southeast corner of Washington State with Cash McCall himself.

All stalwart Presbyterians the McCalls were, as were my own forebears, and to see the wife of young Ted McCall, who had the responsibility of guiding the McCall interests into the modern era, to see his wife out engaging in what appeared to be moon worship? The conservative, Halprin side of my brain was scandalized, while my inner wild child hissed: "Millie, babe, go for it."

Perhaps this explained what Millie McCall was doing here in the San Juan Islands, sheltered as they are from the open ocean by the Olympic mountain range, and flanked to the north by the enormous Vancouver Island. Millie McCall wouldn't be the first heiress stashed by her family here in these lovely but protected islands, far from the prying eyes of her socialite peers with their highly structured pecking order, their cotillions, tea parties, charity balls, church fund-raisers and golf outings. For a socialite of the eighties, Harley riding was not likely to be considered an appropriate pursuit.

Out there on Indian Island, Millie McCall made a spectacle of herself, twirling slowly around, raising her arms wide to embrace the moon, holding her pose so long I grew tired of watching her. When I next looked back to this speck of an island, Millie was gone and it took me a few minutes to see that she was approaching along the land bridge. The tide was rising by this time and the waves lapped at her Doc Martens. There was a ritualistic quality to Millie's stride, and then I realized that the step she was doing was the wedding march. Rather than rush out to escort her as I had planned to do, I stepped back into the shadows of the porch and let her glide right past me. The moon gleamed on her face and her eyes were fixed ahead and her lips moved in silent chat, but the amazing thing was, her face was now composed; the tic was gone. In repose, Millie McCall was a classic beauty, fine of bone and feature, her face as delicately balanced as a tulip on a long and graceful stem of a neck.

Larry Fenton and Bob Hamer came rushing out the door, their clamor startling Millie out of her ritual.

"Millie, it has been wonderful," Larry said. "I hate to leave but Betsy is frantic. Our baby is burning with fever."

"You go on, Larry. We'll do this again. Next time, I'll clean you out."

"Goodnight dear, I'm going with Larry," Bob said, pecking her on the cheek. "I'm Larry's little girl's godfather." Panicked, I blurted that I'd serve them as a runner on my Harley, fetching doctor, drugs, firewood, food, prescriptions, or whatever else Larry's family needed.

Larry clapped me on the shoulder, winking as he said: "What Bob and I need you to do, Jim, is to see that Millie enjoys her night out and gets home safely." The wink pissed me off. Was the sick baby just an excuse? These two guys were doing just what Ben told me to do, get out of the game while the getting was good.

"Look what I've done," Millie wailed. "My boots are soaked and covered with mud. I can't track sand into the Inn and ruin Todd's new flooring. He'd never forgive me." She sat down on the cast iron bench on the porch. She was trembling all over and I was alarmed. Millie seemed to be in the early stages of shock. "Jim, I've some slippers in the right-hand pocket of my saddlebag. Would you be a dear and get them? And would you please bring me the red velvet bag?"

A red velvet bag? Of course. The eccentric Mrs. Millie McCall was just another big sister. Nine sisters and a demanding mother I had, who were forever sending me off on some errand or other. Fetch for the lady I could do. I retrieved her velvet bag and her slippers for her. When her own trembling fingers could not unlace the swollen leather thongs of her Doc Martens, I did the honors. I pried her feet free of her soggy boots and peeled off her sopping socks. I'd brought along my good cashmere scarf from my own saddle pouch and used that to dry her feet and I warmed them and massaged them as I knew to do, her narrow, bony feet in my big hands. Millie's eyes closed and she made these low moans that were…that were…effusive, to say the least.

"Oh. Jim. What bliss. I never knew that feet could feel so…"

The slippers glittered in the moonlight, sliver things with spangles on them and I slid them on her feet, and helped her up and she leaned into me as I ushered her through the door and into a wing chair close to the fire. I stirred the fire to life. How to make a drowsy fire roar was a skill I'd learned from Ben Bridges. I made Millie sip some water and went out to talk to Todd Fircloth, who was hovering in the hall.

"Mrs. McCall's had a bit of a shock, wading in the tide. I've rubbed some warmth back into her, but her shoes are too flimsy to hold the heat. Find her a floor pillow, would you? Or a hot water bottle, if you have one."

A waiter arrived immediately with a footstool, a hot water bottle and a fur throw for milady. I bundled Millie's feet into my cashmere scarf and left her to doze by the fire. I waited until she breathed deeply, whereupon I decided I could flee. I took my leather jacket from the back of my chair, only to find that the extra chairs had been removed, and a fresh deck had been laid. The bar waiter delivered a pair of hot drinks, the house version of the Brandy Alexander, a sweetly lethal concoction known simply as: Lookout!

Millie roused herself, flinging off her blanket, ditching the cashmere scarf twined around her feet and wriggling her toes in the pliable slippers. Ten minutes earlier the lady had seemed half dead. Now she brimmed with energy as she summoned me to the table. This Millie McCall was another woman entirely. The false eyelash had disappeared from her eyelid. She was made up to perfection, the blush, the painted lips, the eyes shadowed just so; her unkempt snarl of wavy hair had been gathered into a sleek chignon. Just where in this scenario Millie had taken a time out to fix herself up, I can't say, but the female tricks I could appreciate, having seen them applied in my own household, and I paid Mrs. McCall the homage she was due, the way Ben Bridges himself would have done: "Millie. You look so fresh, so beautiful."

"Thank you Jim, she said. "Praise be to the full moon." She

stretched her fingers toward me, her polished red nails. There's nothing like a dose of moonbeams to refresh a girl."

"So that's what you were doing, primping out there on the atoll?"

"Absorbing lunar energy," Millie said. "I suffer from a chemical imbalance, you know."

"I didn't. I'm sorry to hear that."

"It's my blessing and my curse. I feel more deeply in the moment; it's so wonderful when I'm on and I have more energy than anyone I know. I'll go and go and go and feel so marvelous, so alive, it's the highest of the highs. I may not sleep for days on end and then I'll come crashing down and be miserable, worse than miserable, so depressed. It's when I start begging to die that drives my dear husband crazy."

"Millie, that's insane," I blurted. *Watch your mouth, idiot.* "I'm sorry, I didn't mean…"

"That's all right, Jim. Insane, nuts, crazy, I've heard it all. That's what all the shrinks tell me, but you see, it really isn't me that makes me feel so awful, it's my chemistry, but all the shots and the pills haven't worked so well for me. There's something about those medicines, they make me feel creepy, as if I don't belong in my own skin."

"So how does the moon figure into the equation?"

"It's a form of yoga."

"It becomes you."

"Thank you, Jim. Such a charming young man. You won't tell anyone what I told you?"

"Of course not."

"Not even Ben?"

"Don't you worry, Mrs. McCall. My grandfather was a country doctor. My father is a pharmacist. No Halprin ever discusses a patient's confidential issues."

"A patient?" she said, her lips drawn down. "Is that what you think of me?"

"Confidentially? I think you are the loveliest, most interesting woman I have ever met. Fascinating." This was my version of Ben Bridges-style blarney, but I felt entitled to it, seeing as how I was standing in for Ben. "But you won't tell anyone I told you?"

Millie laughed at that, laughed until tears came into her dark eyes, which in this light were a deep sea blue, and I laughed as well, and then Millie turned to business.

"Cards?" she said. "Cards help me focus when I'm feeling high."

"Fine," I said. "Your pleasure, Ma'am."

"Gin rummy," she said.

Only two players, no place to hide. I didn't dare lose Ben's money, so I focused on those cards. Drank two or three of those Lookouts! On the sly, of course, when Todd Fircloth wasn't looking. Slowed down my thinking. Stared holes in those cards. This had to be the slowest game of gin rummy on the planet, but Millie didn't seem to notice.

Millie, for all her newly acquired lunar energy, didn't have the cards maybe? My thinking was somewhat blurry by then? All I know is, a pile of chips accumulated on my side of the table. Ben's stake was growing exponentially and I was having a fine time.

It was coming up on one a.m. Todd Fircloth, doing his best to suppress his weariness, offered Millie a second Lookout! Possibly this was one drink too many. Suddenly Millie went on the attack: "Well, Todd, tell me about that your dealer of yours. Who is this Miss Olympia?"

"Lovely, isn't she?" Fircloth kissed his fingers and waggled them in the air.

"A poker dealer dressed in Valentino? Or Victor Costa at the least," Millie snarled. "Not on this island."

Fircloth laughed. "Nothing gets past you, does it, Millie."

"One of Ted's plants, is she?" Todd gave me the eye. I vacated my chair. He seated himself and pulled close to Millie. "Trust me, Millie. She is not."

"She's a spy in designer duds."

Todd grimaced as he shook his head. "Millie, that's your own paranoia talking. Your husband has nothing to do with this. The girl's real name is Marion Walton. She's my ex-wife's niece. She'll be the dining room hostess at the Inn for the summer."

"Where did she come up with the shuffle?"

"Marion's dad Harvey built The Horseshoe Club in Las Vegas with some spare change left over from his inherited oil money. Mom is eyeing a top rung on the social ladder for her only daughter. She insisted on shipping Marion off to a Swiss finishing school so as to wash the gambling taint off her, but it hasn't worked so far. Cards are in her blood."

Millie's face relaxed. "You wouldn't lie to me?"

"Come on, sweetie, let's catch some air." Todd coaxed Millie to her feet and walked her out through the door. I asked for a refill on the coffee I'd been drinking by the gallon for the last few hours. I was exhausted. I had to call it a night soon. I was supposed to be back at work as a camp counselor on Sucia Island by tomorrow afternoon, and this was a prized job I'd aced other kids out of, on account of my dad was in his third term in the state legislature. Never mind that I was pulling strings that hizzoner himself didn't know I'd pulled. He hated that sort of thing. Dad and I weren't exactly seeing eye-to-eye.

When Todd returned with Millie, they were pals again. They hugged. They kissed. We exited the Inn through the back door toward the off the street parking, where Millie had left her bike beside mine. I'd figured her for a sleek low-rider, but her Harley was bigger than mine, a heavier touring model with an oversized bagger compartment on the back.

"An FLT?"

"FHLT," she said, "smoother than any touring bike I've ever had."

"Equipped with a CB? Far out. Did it ever give you any trouble?"

"That was the FLT," Millie said. "I had one of the first ones of those. I thought I was so cool, talking to the truckers, until I stalled out in the desert and had to flag a trucker with my thumb."

"And not your knee?"

Millie's reply was a glint of straight white teeth in the dark. "What? And unlace my Doc Martens? I wasn't so desperate as that. Come to find out, the CD caused some sort of mechanical glitch on a few of the early FLTs. I traded up as soon as I could. I do love these new engines with the five speed transmissions, don't you?"

"What will yours do?"

"Top speed is 105 mph on the straight. My favorite ride on Orcas is the switchbacks down from Mt. Constitution. Have you done that ride?"

"Maybe a few hundred times, but never over 90."

Millie laughed at this bald exaggeration. Her laugh was a sort of purr, a sound like a sack of river stones muffled in a velvet bag.

"Lady, you are out of sight," I blurted, before I had the sense to keep my mouth shut. We'd been standing in the shadows of the back porch, admiring our bikes and ourselves, or at least that's my take on it. One of the shadows winked out over by Millie's bike and that's when I noticed we had company.

A couple of guys were hanging over Millie's Harley. They didn't see us, concealed as we were by the overhang of the back porch, our voices drowned out by the music from the bar. A flashlight played over the elegant seat of Millie's machine and lingered on the conchos plastered all over her bike. I saw the flash of a knife and a black hole where a concho had been.

"Stay right here," I muttered. "Don't you move. I'll take care of this." In four strides I was on top of the pair. I grabbed the one with the flashlight by the scruff of his neck and tripped the one attempting to run off with a canvas bag. He grunted as he hit the pavement, then rolled to one side and made an attempt to scramble after the shiny contents of the bag. Conchos rolled every which way accompanied by their own tinkling music. I flattened that one with a boot to the middle of his back.

"Hey man, get off me," he squawked.

Mr. Flashlight twisted around and shot the beam into my eyes. I could see his angry eyes as he sent shards of pain into my brain and I let up the pressure on the guy underfoot, who scrambled to his feet and started to run.

I locked Mr. Flashlight into a chokehold. The light dropped out of his hand and rolled into the shrubbery, where it lit up a fat white blossom on the Inn's prize rhododendron bushes as if it was the only flower on the planet.

From the road I heard a single siren note, the slamming of a car door and a barked command: "Police. Freeze."

I awakened out of a sleep, perhaps a dream. Or was it a trance? What I had seen—or sensed—was that the room I was lying in was breathing. At the corners of the room the walls pulsed, and they did so as well where the pitched ceiling opened and closed with rhythmic inhalations, revealing the white lights of the stars against a night sky that was black as marble and totally cloudless. Where was I? What happened to the moonlight?

Whether I had experienced a deeper vision of the universe I cannot say even now. I hoped that is what it was because there was nothing at all frightening about this experience, it was very pleasant, very benign and for all the traumatic events of my night shepherding Millie McCall around, it was this singular vision that she offered me—in the form of a small white pill—that has remained with me for all these years.

Back then, however, I was more concerned with the time, close to three a.m. I found myself sprawled across a musty smelling and lumpy bed covered with an old quilt, very good needlework as I saw through my mother's trained eye, but so worn the stuffing dribbled out. Here I was out with Millie, miles away from the McCall estate, on the crest of a mountainous knob locally as Turtle Head. I was sprawled on top of the bed in one of the back bedrooms in a house that we had broken into—or Millie had—several hours earlier, and the bizarre events of the evening came flooding back.

After the altercation with what proved to be two juvenile prowlers outside the Lookout Inn, we had started off on our Harleys, Millie leading the way out of Eastsound Village, taking a sedate and quiet trip along the shoreline on an easterly course which would lead to the McCall estate. For awhile we rode along behind the deputy who had the miscreants in the backseat of his cruiser.

Once the kids were handcuffed and hauled away, Millie was inclined to laugh the whole thing off. She had signed the police report, but I wondered whether she would press charges, even though we had had to spend a good forty minutes or so rounding up the silver doodads that the kids had pried off her Harley, and the damage to her custom bike was extensive.

"They were after trophies," she dumped the trinkets into her saddlebag, "a piece of the McCalls."

"But Millie. You have to take a stand here. You have to nail these two before every other kid on the island comes looking for conchos off your bike."

"Oh I suppose so," Millie snorted. "You sound just like Ted. You men are all alike."

"Yeah, baby," I said, and what's good about you women is—you are not alike, especially yours truly, Mrs. McCall."

At that point I became aware of the plinking of the tinny upright piano we had discovered in a corner of the living room, and I heard Millie singing in a quavering Piaf-style voice that drew me off the musty bed. I stood behind the bedroom door, taking care to keep the weight off my throbbing leg, rubbing a cramp out of my neck and suppressing a sneeze, as I listened to Millie doing Piaf songs. Millie played very well and her gargly voice was a good fit for the Piaf vibrato.

I was still in my jeans and chaps but my leather jacket was hung over an iron bedpost and my swollen leg hurt like a bitch.

A roaring fire I'd built in the stone fireplace had dispelled the musty odor of a house damp with disuse. Millie banged on the badly tuned piano, swaying to the sound of her own voice, a thin trail of smoke from one of her pencil-thin cigars rose from an ashtray beside her on the piano bench.

The heat from the fireplace blasted me, and so it was no wonder that Millie, laboring at her music beside the fireplace, had flung off her motorcycle jacket and dumped it on the floor, had stripped out of her filmy red nightgown, leaving the firelight to burnish rosy highlights across her plump white shoulders, bare breasted she was, bare everything. I was aroused at the white, fleshy sight of her, found myself wanting her, and I was fascinated, but also horrified.

After all, it was plain to me that for all her dalliances, her poker parties and whatnot, that Millie McCall belonged to her powerful husband, and if my existence in her life was ever known to Ted McCall at all, I could be crushed like some unwary fly smacked by a swatter. Never mind my ancient family tie to Cash McCall himself, which his great-grandson had probably never heard about.

It stood to reason by the light of the full moon that Mrs. McCall's dangerous exuberance would be well known to her husband and that in his frequent absences, he would have servants and a security detail in place to keep a watch on her. That's why, I now realized, the law had arrived so promptly back at the Lookout Inn where the kids were plucking conchos off her bike.

After that incident, it was coming back to me how we had ridden sedately out of the Village heading due east toward the McCall estate, where a frantic search for Mrs. McCall might now be underway, since we should have long ago arrived back at the McCall mansion.

I feared that the reverse route, which Millie had finagled me into, was her means of dodging her keepers. Once the deputies had passed us and were well out of sight, Millie, riding ahead of me, veered northward via Prune Alley. She screeched to a halt at the parking lot of the Pit Stop. We were greeted by the catcalls of a few stragglers from the bars who were thrilled to see Millie, their heroine, and they all cheered and hooted as she swaggered past, the fun-loving heiress who knew them all by name and called out to them as she made her way into the crowded aisles of the Island version of the mom & pop market. Where most of the clients were loading up on more beer, Millie's purchase was a box of the ladylike cigars she favored. She thanked the proprietor, Dorothy Mudgett, for stocking them for her.

"Don't you worry none, Miz Millie," Dorothy said, her gat-toothed grin spreading across her wizened face. "All the ladies on the island are ordering them—strictly on the q.t., a course."

From The Pit Stop we had ridden west on Dovecote and hung left into Lookout Lane, putting us right back where we had started, alongside the Inn. At that point we should have turned east on the Horseshoe Highway that runs along the sound, but Millie outfoxed me again, swinging due west. She stomped on the gas and roared off.

A twisting and leaping chase ensued, and it is a good thing the moon was high when we reached the wooded tract at the north end of Crow Valley, a few miles west of Eastsound. I missed one of the hairpin turns and slid clear across the road, taking a flying leap toward a steep embankment where I might well have broken my own stupid neck in a direct hit on one of the monster old growth Douglas firs, as wide as the columns on some European cathedral, and quite possibly a seedling when Columbus discovered America.

I took a screeching, last minute slide into unstable gravel, flattened a roadside marker and lay my own bike on its side, raking my right leg in the process, but I was saved from more serious injury by my heavy leathers. Badly shaken, leg burning, I started off behind Millie, whose own headlights were lost to me. There was nowhere to ride but for a few side roads down dark lanes to various farmsteads and so I figured I'd eventually meet up with her somewhere on the Horseshoe highway, reckoning by this time that my own chase of her at high speed was compounding her recklessness.

Millie must have heard me coming along. I saw her flashlight signaling an SOS, slowed down and found myself on the broad and gated logging road up the side of Turtleback Mountain. Millie had parked right beside the Private Property/No Trespassing Sign.

"What took you?"

"A wipeout."

"A deer?"

"You might say that." An encounter with a passing deer is the most acceptable and unverifiable scenario any Islander may offer for a given mishap. It is impossible to reside in the San Juans without having several close calls with a wandering deer in any given season.

"You hurt?"

"Just a touch."

"Really?" She ran her flashlight down my leg, and sucked in her breath when she saw my ripped chaps. "Show me."

"Best offer I've had today, but sorry, I forgot to shave."

"Cut the crap, Jim. Let's see."

Hoisting the chaps didn't hurt so much but peeling my torn jeans off my shin was a pain, revealing a nasty burn embedded with gravel.

"We've got to take care of that," Millie said. "Come on, I know a place."

"You would."

I expected we'd turn right around and head back to Eastsound, but that would be too simple for Millie. Instead we started up the posted logging trail, riding at first, but recent rains and the deep ruts carved in the road by logging trucks made the road impassable.

When we came to a recent deadfall, an enormous Doug fir uprooted across the road, I told Millie that we were turning back. Instead, she insisted we were nearly there, to what she referred to as the Blysdale House, and I realized where she meant for us to visit—one of the underground legends on the island. I'll admit right now that my curiosity got the better of me, which is how I became Millie's unwitting co-conspirator. Well, okay, make that a half-wit co-conspirator.

The trail was steep enough that I was breathing hard and my shin complained with every step. I considered myself lucky that my ankle felt a bit puffy but not broken, or I wouldn't have made it at all, and I was having increasing difficulty putting weight on my leg. As it was, Millie was neither winded nor complaining. She galloped along, doing her salutes to the moon at every turn of the road where any bright patch of light presented itself like a spotlight in a darkened theater.

"The Blysdale house," I said. "So that's what it's called? I believe I've heard of it—by reputation, but I never would have guessed the Blysdale family owned it." Blysdale was the second half of the renowned Canadian timber outfit, O'Donovan Blysdale.

"Oh really?" Millie said. Her eyes went wide.

"A house on the mountain, abandoned by the owner for years but known to travelers of the hippie era," I said.

"How did you hear about it?" Millie blurted, confirming my suspicion that the tales I'd heard were true.

"Ben's tree guy, told me. You know the one-handed arborist? He leads the Earth Day parade on stilts."

"Gabriel Steed?"

"Gabe told me there's an old house up here on Turtleback, not far off the trail up to where the stone anchor lies, but the way is hidden so that most people never find it."

Millie stared at me, and by the light of the moon I saw her smirk, and so I described what I had heard. "I'm talking about a one story cedar house with a shake roof built at the edge of a beaver pond. There's a fine view of the Canadian San Juans, a couple of bedrooms with the furniture still in it, a good fireplace and a decent library of books."

Millie smiled, took my arm. The whites of her eyes glinted out from the dark shadow of her face. That I knew about this legendary house raised my status in her eyes.

"Go on."

"If you travel in the right circles, and are deemed trustworthy, it might be that you are told how to get into the house. If you do stay, you have a duty to do something to keep the place in good repair, and to leave it in order for the next wayfarer."

"There's a guestbook, a sort of journal, where travelers record their thoughts, or note anything unusual about the birds or animals they observe."

Millie merely smiled, her lips barely turned up: "Or any other unusual doings."

"So Millie? I take it you have been a guest of Blysdale House?"

"Jimmy Blysdale adored me," Millie said, averting her eyes, "but as far as I was concerned, we were just good friends. That is all it ever was, just friends. I never led Jimmy on. Never."

My leg was dragging by this time, which Millie noticed. "All right," she said. "We'll be taking a rugged trail soon, if I remember the way."

"*If* doesn't cut it, Millie. *If* you don't know where we're going, we turn back."

"We'll stop right here. I'll reconnoiter while you take a rest."

I wanted to protest but was completely fagged. I took a seat on a rock and waited while Millie trudged on up the trail. I watched the beam of her flashlight sweep the trail in front of me and then disappear around a bend. For five or ten minutes I could hear her on the trail, but I was left alone with nothing to listen to but the creak and rattle of the timber in a light breeze. I probably dozed off. All I recall is that when Millie returned, flashing her light into my dazed eyes, she caught me with my teeth chattering. I was having hot flashes and cold chills.

"You poor boy. That leg is killing you."

We finally reached the house via a miserable quarter mile of a deer trail that dropped down a steep incline. I had to hobble from tree to tree, using a stick as a cane. A small lake appeared, round as a silver coin, shining in the moonlight, the dark outline of the house, the windows barred. I was all in. I stumbled over a root and landed on my bad leg, sending bolts of pain up my spine. Millie helped me limp to the porch steps where I sat while she went round to the back door to find the key and let me in.

Piaf had been dead for a couple of decades on the August night of Millie's poker party. Considering the lame piano, Millie did well by Edith, and I hovered behind the bedroom door for a long time, under Millie's spell. Thanks to my older sisters, who knew every line of every Piaf tune, I knew enough French to recognize the medley Millie had woven together, *La Foule*, a lover glimpsed in a crowd but lost in the fray; *Padam, Padam, Padam*, Paris, Paris, Paris. I followed the lyrics of these first two songs, but it was when Millie launched into *Le Vie in Rose*, life in the pink, the high life, that I forgot my own self-consciousness and limped into the room and stood with my back to my own roaring fire.

"But, Millie, for you it should be life in the red, wouldn't you say?" Millie laughed and changed the words to Le Vie en Rouge.

I'd fried my backside by this time and my leg was aching, so I sat down on the sagging sofa covered with an old Army blanket and found on a coffee table, hewn from a plank and lacquered over, the legendary journal, the pen set out, an invitation for me to add my own account of the breathing house I'd witnessed. An entry in the journal in this underground house would be my admission ticket to all that was artsy and hip and cultivated here in the San Juans where you had to be a card-carrying character just to count as a resident. Instead, I found myself reading Millie's entry:

"I believe all who visit Blysdale house must know that it has been left here for lost wayfarers by the will of Jimmy's mother, Mary Alice Blysdale. She encouraged Jimmy to follow his love for photography and poetry. Jimmy was an artist, but his father couldn't accept that. He wanted a son who would follow his footsteps in business, but Jimmy rejected the entire timber industry as an obscene assault on the environment.

On the night of his death, Jimmy dived into the quarry pond and never came up. That was the night a bunch of us had sneaked out of camp to smoke dope and drink beer, and I am ashamed to say that Jimmy caught Ted McCall and me necking on a blanket on the quarry's canyon side…that cliff, that cliff he dived from…so steep, so high…."

Millie sang, now, "Why, Jimmy, why? Why so steep, so high?"

The playing stopped. Millie came to the sofa and I sat rooted to the spot by the ample folds of her baby white skin and her jaunty breasts just begging to be caressed.

"How are you feeling, Jim," she purred, but as she put her hands on my chest and offered her lips to be kissed, I saw that the tic had returned to her face, and had an inkling that I was just a strand-in for the hapless Jimmy Blysdale, so I pecked her on the forehead and slid away from her, hating myself for my own cowardice in doing so.

"I'm having fever chills again, Millie, so let me stoke the fire." There was enough wood left to keep the coals going for awhile, and the fire was laboring under the weight of the new wood, creating a momentary chill, which gave me the excuse to hand Millie her red nightgown. She sat on the sagging couch looking very irritated in the silky but bedraggled folds, her gown singed here and there from her Harley's hot exhaust.

"We need some coffee, don't you think?" I hobbled into the kitchen using my stick for balance. I was having real difficulty putting any weight on my leg by this time. Millie's backpack was open. I found some packets of tea, located a grimy kettle, rinsed it as best I could, and filled it with bottled water from Millie's pack. I set the kettle on the gas range, found a match, and amazingly enough the burner came alight. Somebody indeed kept this place running.

Millie had set out a packet of cream cheese, some Spam, a couple of bananas, some hard rolls. I was ravenous, thrilled to see some food, but I also realized that Millie had planned this whole episode. She intended to drag me up here, or any of the other poker players she could snare, maybe Eyepatch Bob, maybe Goldeneye Fenton.

As the tea water steamed to life in the kettle, dawn ripened like a fruit, lush colors fading in. Through the kitchen window I could see a couple of beavers working on their dam at the edge of the lake. A chorus of ducks and geese honked in the new dawn. Millie had returned to the piano and launched to our swan song for the night, *"Non Je ne Regrette Rien,"* I regret nothing, and I set two cups of coffee down on the piano and sang along with her, where she sat, her nightgown covered by a moth-eaten bathrobe. Millie rose, slipped her arms around my waist, and I glanced down at her eyes, blue as bruises, face puffy from lack of sleep, this lost girl/woman, her pale skin washed pink in the morning light, and she was as delectable, vulnerable, and lovely as she was unapproachable, at least by the likes of me.

"This is Jimmy Blysdale's old bathrobe," Millie said and I didn't want to hear how it was that she knew for a fact just whose robe it was. At that point I was relieved to hear a rumbling loud enough to shake the house.

"Loggers," I said. "Maybe we can catch a ride down the mountain."

Millie's face froze, her mouth drew down. "Dammed Wads. I just wish for once she would mind her own business."

"Wads?"

Whatever Millie said was drowned out by a deafening roar that shook the place.

"Whoa. Nice of them to leave us with a roof."

"That's Sully for you. That showoff."

"Sully?"

"Andy Sullivan, the chopper pilot for fire and rescue."

"We're being rescued?"

"*You* are being rescued. *I* am being captured. I want you to hobble into the bedroom, prop up that leg and look like something a dog wouldn't eat for breakfast."

"Hey Millie, you didn't have to call out a chopper on my account."

"Go. I have to toddle up the side of that rise out there and do the white flag routine."

"I don't get it."

"Puh-leeze, Jim. Trust me. You can't walk."

"Truth is I can't." I had to laugh. Millie's keepers were after her and she was using me as her excuse for failing to report in at the mansion.

She grabbed me around the waist and hustled me to the bedroom. She yanked back the covers.

"Don't you move. I'm sure your leg is broken." I settled onto the bed. Millie propped my leg up on a bedroll made from lumpy pillows.

"I'll go out and flag them—tell them I'm thrilled they're here to fly you off."

"Hey, Millie? I'm thrilled even if you aren't."

I heard the front door slam, pictured Millie McCall rushing up the steep hill behind the house in Jimmy Blysdale's bathrobe, whereupon I suffered a moment of panic. Sudden death might be preferable to Millie's rescuers finding her here with me. No doubt her husband would know all about our interlude.

I couldn't see much of the action from the side window of the bedroom but what I heard was chaotic. The beavers on the dam skedaddled with slaps of their tails. A flock of Canadian geese took off with frantic, yodeling honks. I glimpsed the chopper as it disappeared behind a hill and came wheeling back around at the top, ready for another pass. At the top of the rise, Millie stood waving her arms overhead, white towel in hand, bare shoulders now fetchingly exposed. Were we surrendering to the authorities? Would we be charged with breaking and entering?

The helicopter landed on the bald top of a rocky plateau, its rotors stirring up dust. The pilot got out, and a second guy with him. They had a stretcher with them, one of those wire baskets used for airlifts. I was thrilled.

Millie threw herself at the pilot, waving her arms. Pointing down at the house, my cue to scrunch down in the sheets and look sick, which was the easy part. I'd banged my sore leg on the edge of the coffee table when Millie rushed me in here and I noticed for the first time that blood was seeping through the rips in my chaps, so I propped it on a clump of bedding made from the decrepit quilt and let her leak.

I heard the front door opened, then slammed, and my rescue squad clumped into the bedroom. The pilot, Andy Sullivan, the same deputy who had rounded up the concho thieves, asked me if I could move. I made him shake me before I opened my eyes and found Sullivan's piercing gaze boring into my dazed one. He asked permission to touch my swollen leg and when he did so I let out such a yelp that he was apparently convinced that I wasn't faking, and believe me, on that part I wasn't.

He grilled Millie about how come she was once again found in the wee hours at Blysdale House and Millie gave some wandering, evasive reply, the gist of which was, she got confused leaving the Lookout Inn and took off in the wrong direction, going a tad fast. She got ahead of me and I spun out trying to catch up.

"With Jim so hurt, Blysdale house was the closest place I could think of to get him off his feet."

Sullivan chuckled sardonically. "Yes ma'am, Blysdale House is the closest place to land a chopper, that is for sure."

The chopper ride to Eastsound village took less than ten minutes. I was loaded into an ambulance at the island's mini airport and driven to the new medical clinic, where Doc Crocker, known by islanders as 'Doc Crock', greeted me over the Ben Franklin style glasses that slid perpetually down his skinny nose.

"Quite a weekend for the BakerVue crew," Doc said. "First Ben Bridges tries suicide by Caterpillar. Now his understudy tries to top the master by riding a Harley over a cliff?"

"The road got away from me, Doc."

Doc peered at me over his glasses. He was adamantly not in favor of Harley riding on the Island. I had first met Doc the time I'd turned twelve and caught a fishhook in the ear. Ben had cut it off with a pair of tin snips and then had Carla bring me to Doc's office for the stitches and the tetanus shot. That was back when Doc Crock was the only physician on the island. Since then well-heeled retirees had by this time discovered The San Juans; the Island now had a fancy medical facility which even has an x-ray machine. Doc cut off his hippie pigtail long ago and turned gray at the temples. As far as I know, Doc no longer grew pot for medicinal purposes in his front yard, but he had developed an owlish stare, which compelled guilty patients to explain their foolish mishaps.

"Look at it this way, Doc. I didn't fly off a cliff and if I had gone over the embankment, it isn't that steep."

"True, Doc said. "So long as you steered clear of the trees."

"You've got a point, Doc."

"And you've got a mangled leg."

Doc's latest intern came waltzing in with a big pair of scissors and a needle filled with something to dull the pain while they peeled me out of my sticky chaps and hacked off my pants leg. The good thing about arriving at the clinic in the wee hours of the morning is, you don't have to wait in line to get into x-ray.

The news was so-so. My femur was cracked, not broken outright and I was lucky that I could bend my knee. Once they had wrapped some three miles of elastic bandage around my leg, Doc ordered me to come back first thing Monday morning.

"I'm working on Sucia Island on Monday. I'm a ranger's assistant."

"If you want to avoid surgery on that leg, you're not working on Sucia on Monday," Doc said. "You'll show up here where we change the dressing on your leg and do another x-ray. You are not to put weight on it."

This was devastating news. I needed the summer job or I couldn't put myself through the fall semester at Western. John J. Halprin had liberated me on my eighteenth birthday, handed me my clothes in a duffle and turned me out of his house. Dad Halprin was one of those sartorially correct churchgoers who disapproved of my scruffy biker lifestyle. I never could convince him that Harley riding was a sport increasingly beloved by hipster professionals.

Millie came in, hovered over me, squeezed my hand, asked me how I felt, but Doc Crock had plans for her.

"All right, Mrs. McCall, let's see how you fared through all this."

"I'm doing fine, Doc. You know I have special powers this time of the lunar cycle."

"So you've said, Mrs. McCall."

"I wouldn't be the first, either, as well you know."

"You wouldn't be the first patient I've heard from who seems to indicate a lunar influence upon his or her health."

"So it's true, Doc?" I blurted, "What's said by cops and crazies?" Millie's eyes widened. "No offense, Millie. I didn't mean you."

"That theory has never been proven in a double blind study so far as I know." Doc stared at Millie over the glasses riding just above his nostrils. "As long as you are here, Mrs. McCall, we may as well do your blood work."

Millie returned with a bandage along her upper arm holding a cotton pad in place. "Jim Halprin, what on earth are you doing in here, lolling around? Come on. Sully has offered to drive us back to pick up our Harleys."

By this time I was high on a cortisone buzz; retrieving our Harleys seemed a fine idea. Sully was a stiff of a guy, whose uniform was so proper his creases creaked when he walked. He helped me into the backseat of his cruiser where I stretched my elasticized leg out straight.

Sully helped Millie into the front seat where she proceeded to babble away, trying to amuse him, but Sullivan was having none of this. He answered her tittle tattle with polite nods.

We stopped briefly where I'd spun out. Sullivan said he'd make a report on it after he dropped us off at the foot of the Turtleback logging road. I protested but he cited regs and that was that.

We'd left our bikes behind one of the old growth firs that had somehow escaped the loggers' saws, probably because Mrs. Blysdale or Mrs. O'Donovan kept an eye on them. Sullivan helped Millie get her bike down to the highway. Then he returned and helped me maneuver my Harley out.

"Might not be such a hot idea to ride with a fat leg, partner," he said. "I'd be happy to do an escort for Ms. McCall. I've got a length of chain in my trunk. We could padlock your bike to a tree and I'll drop you off wherever you say."

"Thanks Sully. I'd hate to tie up the Island's finest. Millie and I will be fine."

A scowl crossed across the deputy's face and I knew what I suspected. Sullivan had the hots for Millie and here I was a green kid implying I had something going with Mrs. McCall. As he left in his cruiser, Sully tipped his hat and spun out, not bothering to wave as he passed Millie, who had started her bike and was riding sedately along the road.

Luckily, my knee was in good shape, and I'd talked Doc Sullivan into packing the heel of my injured foot in enough leverage to make riding possible. I had gotten my second wind and was feeling no pain. It was one of those warm, mid-August mornings in the islands that promised a fine day, and I felt that I might as well seize the moment and ride, while the riding was good. I'd put out of my mind the uncomfortable thought that I might have to sacrifice my interest in the Harley if I intended to go back to college in September.

Third turn through the woods we passed Sullivan running a tape on my skid marks. He was making a diagram, all right. A road marker I'd flattened lay in the dirt. He could charge me with assault on county property if he felt like it, but what if he did? It was darker than pitch when I hit that stretch of the road and the county was about six years behind in painting the center line. Of course, I'd have to lean on Dad's attorney to make a case, if there was one, and I was on the outs with the Honorable John J. Halprin, which made such a scenario somewhat awkward.

Millie honked and treated Sullivan to a back-handed wave, which he ignored, pretending to concentrate on his work, so I sanctioned his rudeness by laying down a big old Harley style fart, leaving him in a cloud of blue fumes.

As we rounded out of the trees, a battered black pickup caught up and passed us in the open curve beside a dilapidated apple barn. It was Eyepatch Bob from last night's poker party. At the top of the rise he stopped at Island Supply and pulled up to one of the antique gas pumps. Millie pulled in behind him and I followed suit, though I simply pulled aside and waited. The only possible turn I could make was on my injured side.

"Millie was doing her usual animated gabbing, hand waving, kissing, hugging, rolling her eyes. Bob filled his pickup, went inside to pay up, and backed his truck past me, motioning me to follow him as he started out on the road. Millie pulled up beside me.

"We're all going to the Lookout Inn for brunch. My treat." At the Inn, we were seated by our dazzling former dealer, Marion Walton, wearing a sophisticated black sheath with a snazzy rhinestone bow closing a diamond-shaped cutout in front. This was a perfect joke, a takeoff on a food service bow tie. As was the fashion at the time, the dress ended way up the thigh. Marion's shapely legs were encased in sheer black stockings with stripes threaded into them. I was blown away and couldn't manage even a Ben-ism by way of complementing her. Millie greeted her with a hug, as if she were a long lost friend, gushing over her dress.

"Another Valentino number? Of course you will be modeling his fall collection?"

"I'm a Victor Costa girl, actually," she said with a bit of an English accent. "I'm too fat to model professionally."

"Well don't let anyone tell you that you aren't just perfect the way you are." Millie, by contrast looked completely disheveled. She went off to the ladies' with her velvet bag, so I had a chance to ogle Marion, but she wasn't taken with my pigtail, Harley rig, and my fat leg. She was polite and civil but not interested and it was Eyepatch Bob who complimented her on her skill at the poker table. He'd shed the "pink medicine" shirt and exchanged it for a Sunday shirt and tie.

"So what happened with Larry Fenton's baby?"

"Doc Crock gave baby Lucy something to get her fever down and the Fentons went off island this morning on the red eye. Doc has ordered further testing at the hospital in Anacortes. He's worried about scarlet fever."

"Oh, Lord."

Millie returned looking more conservative than I had ever seen her. She wore an oversized tee that covered her clear down over her bottom, clinging to her curvy body. The ruffled red nightgown beneath became a skirt that demurely swathed her knees. She'd ditched the overblown lashes that would have done better on a Guernsey and applied a little rouge to her stark face. She had gathered her raggedy shoulder length hair into a pony tail and for the moment, her tic was in abeyance.

Millie seemed to know everyone who stopped in to load up on Todd Fircloth's elaborate Sunday spreads featuring the menacing food that threatens to choke off every artery in America, except maybe for the Holland Tunnel.

I gloried in my steroid high and managed to drink an entire pot of the coffee that Todd kept in insulated pitchers on the table, to ease the burden of the army of waitresses the Inn kept on the payroll in high season.

"What's with your leg?" Bob waved a biscuit dripping homemade blackberry jam in my direction.

"Had a close encounter with a road marker."

"Should you be riding at all?"

"I should avoid spinning out, that's for sure."

Breakfast dragged on for an hour or more. We had a hard time getting back on the road again, seeing as how the entire Island seemed to be aware that Millie had gone missing from her own poker night and people kept stopping by to say hello to her. A few people who knew me asked after Ben, and a couple of my mother's elderly friends gave me the fish eye over my choice of wardrobe. Or was it my pigtail that bothered them? Or maybe the Fu Manchu moustache?

We managed to leave just as the traffic from the ten a.m. arrival hit the main drag and we had to wait for the parade.

Millie got honked at every fourth car or so, while I was gauging when we could get into traffic. The Horseshoe Highway, the island's main road, curves down a rise before it comes through town. That was why I noticed the stunning vehicle bringing up the rear. A four-seater convertible with the top down, cream in color, an enormous steepled grille, and massive headlights caked in chrome.

"Whoa. Look at that. What is it? A Rolls? A Bentley?"

"Rolls? Where?" Millie stood on tiptoes, shielding her eyes from the sun to look where I pointed. "Oh. My. God." She flung herself into my arms.

"Millie? What is it?"

"Hide me."

I wrapped my arms around her, sheltering her face from the road. But for my fat leg I could have grabbed her and made for the trail down to the beach. Best I could do on no notice was, I stuck her head into my jacket and pushed my face over the top of her head, as if we were locked in a passionate embrace with our backs to the road. Sadly, the traffic was heavy both directions, what with the church crowds coming into the intersection further along. Summer people, not so familiar with four way stops out here in the wilderness, created a drag. I found myself peering up from my passion just as the glory car rolled toward us.

As it came alongside, I kept Millie's head pinned into my shoulder and glanced up to get the impression of a stunning woman in the front seat, her head wrapped in a silk scarf I could read as Hermes by a mile, a skill instilled in me by my well-dressed sisters. She wore sunglasses big as saucers.

On the rear passenger side was a blasé male face that I knew I knew. Or thought I should know, at least. A smashing blonde sat next to him, her hair whipping in the breeze. As the car swept past, I raised my head and caught a glance of the driver's face in the rear view mirror; I thought I read a flicker of recognition in the expression and also—and also… what? Disgust?

"Has he gone?" Millie murmured into my chest.

"Who?"

"Ted." Of course. The cool convertible. The beautiful people. The California plates. Millie squirmed out of my embrace. "Do you think he saw us?"

"I doubt it." *So why the sneer?*

Millie muttered under her breath. Just what she was saying to herself I didn't catch, but she seemed to be contrite, appalled, blaming herself. Once the Rolls was clear through town, she headed for Gasoline Alley, the main drag version of the Pit Stop. It was fancier, carried the Seattle dailies and the *New York Times*, a selection of decent wines and upscale deli cheeses with French names and outta sight price tags. Millie was friends with the manager as it turned out, who let her use the phone in the office.

Millie tossed me a credit card and asked me to gas up the hogs. When the station attendant saw the bandage on my leg, he waved me off and took over for me. The steroid shot was beginning to wear off, so I hopped over to a cast iron bench between pots of geraniums where people went to smoke, and elevated my leg on one of the pots. The office window happened to be open and I heard Millie's voice.

"I forgot, Wads," Millie sobbed. "Ted will be so disappointed in me...Of course I didn't mean...It was an accident, Wads....I am listening...I know you do....What?...Ted wants me to....Yes." Her tone was soft, defeated. She cut off the conversation with a click of the receiver. I stood up and hobbled over to my Harley, arms crossed, eyes on the street, looking for something worthy of the pretense I meant to establish.

Millie signed her tab, and handed the attendant an embarrassingly large tip. Her eyes were red. "Is something wrong, Millie?"

"So Ted's arrived with yet another carload of...ah...friends...and I forgot about it, yes, I'm late to uh, whatever we were supposed to do today."

"So? Let's get you on the move."

"I'm not wanted."

"What?"

"Wads has moved my things to The Crow's Nest."

"Wads?"

"The housekeeper, Stella Wadsworth. She's a retired Army nurse and she's in charge. Wads runs my house like a barracks."

"And this Crow's..."

"It's the guest house. I'm being punished. I've been a bad girl. To bed without supper. No stars. No movie."

"Stars as in Hollywood?"

"Shhhhh. Nobody on the island is to know. It's why these people come here. They want to hide where they won't be recognized."

"Fat chance."

"Well. At least they won't be made over. Islanders don't gush."

"This is true."

"Ted's their lackey. I hate it."

"Really?"

Millie rubbed her fingers together. "They want Ted's money, of course. These people want Ted to bail out some movie."

"So what, Millie? Ted could make a fortune."

"Or lose one," Millie said, swinging her leg over the saddle. "Yes the McCalls are old money but Ted likes to let them think that he's the next Howard Hughes," she said. "Come on, Jim, Let's catch up to them. Some road movie for females this is. They want to see road action? I'll show them."

Millie slipped gracefully into the slow moving traffic. She was four car lengths ahead of me before I could manage to hobble over to my bike. By the time I had worked my way awkwardly into traffic, Millie had passed through town and hung a right, eastward toward the Rosario estate and this Foxglove mansion I'd heard Millie was so proud of. She was ten cars ahead of me, fifteen by the time we reached the second hairpin curve around the cliffs.

The Saturday traffic was slow, to her advantage, and as I looked down across the valley at Ship Bay, I saw the Rolls disappear around a bend. Millie rode his tail, though Ted gave no sign at all that he was aware of what his wife was up to. As for me, I plodded along, taking no chances. My fat shin ballooned against its bindings; my squishy ankle ached, letting me know it was time for a rest.

Just why I was tagging along behind the two McCalls was the subject of a fierce internal debate. My sensible, responsible, John J. Halprin side told me that it was high time to quit and go home, home as represented by the BakerVue Lodge. I had a job to do. Ben and Carla Bridges would be worrying about me by now. On the other hand, my Ben Bridges' Wild Child was quick to note: You are done for, buddy. You are out for the count, man. You've wrecked your leg, dude, put yourself out of a job for the summer. You might as well tag along here with what amounts to the Island A-List, for the sake of whatever opportunities—or adventures—might present themselves.

I'd lost sight of both Millie and Rolls long before I passed beneath the quaint arch that marks the beginning of the Moran State Park, where the topography changed. The park is heavily forested in old growth timber and the road runs along Cascade Lake, a pristine mountain lake with a sandy beach near the entrance. The park is packed to capacity this time of year because it's one of the few places on the Island where parents can take the kids for a swim. The campgrounds are booked ahead for months at a time. I didn't think the lake would hold much interest for jaded celebrity types, but I was wrong. Ahead of me, the Rolls was parked at the very edge of the lake. Ms. Hermes was out of the car, taking a close-up shot of a tiny island deer, a doe trotting across the road followed by her two dappled fawns.

Ted McCall could have told his lovely guest that the grounds of his mansion would be overrun with these same deer, tame as dogs. Island deer graze the blooms right out of the gardens and will eat out of your hand, or maybe nibble your fingers off if they are hungry enough. Not polite, I suppose, since he sat staring ahead, his elbow cocked on the driver's side door, his head propped on his closed fist. He may not have noticed the motley figure of his wife on her motorcycle, hovering in the trees a few car lengths behind him. I pulled up beside Millie.

"What's happening?"

"Ted's playing games." She lifted her helmet and ran a hand through the damp nest of her unruly mane, her fingers plowing up her black roots.

The cutie with the camera pranced back to the Rolls, handed her Polaroid shot to the female in the backseat. Ted turned his head back in our direction as he waited for an opening in traffic, and I felt a flicker of recognition. The McCalls were doing their best to outfox each other.

"So, Millie, it's high time for me to split. You'll catch up with Ted. I have to get back to BakerVue. Carla Bridges will need me to…"

"Jim, dear, get real. I need you right now. I'm in terrible trouble. Yes, of my own making, it is true, but then again, there was a serious medical problem, you know, and when Wads sees such a nice young person as you, she won't be hissy with me anymore."

The Rolls squeezed into traffic in front of an island-style jalopy full of teens, kids no doubt thrilled to halt for the dazzling coupe. Millie revved her bike and waved frantically for me to keep up. She sped into the stream of traffic moving around the lake, but I couldn't get my clunky leg back into position soon enough and the next opening was a good ten cars down the line. Last I saw of them, Millie was right on Ted's tail, her red nightgown flapping behind her like a warning flag, to which all passengers in the Rolls seemed oblivious. An afternoon breeze had come up and the ladies in the vehicle had put on enormous hats which blocked out any views of Millie running right behind them.

The trip around Cascade Lake was a drag. Pedestrians ambled across the road. Clumsy boat trailers backed into traffic and took their sweet time getting themselves organized. Teens stopped to hang out the doors of their cars, talking to their buddies. Bicycle riders swooped through the traffic with irritating nonchalance.

Once the park was behind, we came to the fork in the road. To the right was the road down to the McCall mansion, which Ben said was on the grounds of Rosario, the old Moran estate. The left fork was the winding highway to the top of Mt. Constitution. I'd started down the right fork to the McCall estate when I heard a Harley revving behind me. I glanced around and there was Millie glaring after me in disgust. I was on the wrong track. I had to wait my turn to cross a single lane bridge, a relic of the Depression era. I swung around and took the right hand turn up the steep highway toward the mountain, but Millie and the Rolls she tailed were already heading out of sight around the first bend.

It was early afternoon. People were still finishing lunch, so that there were few takers heading for the mountain top, and so I gunned my engine and let her rip. Okay, so I let her amble is more like it. Now and again I would catch glimpses of the two McCalls speeding up the winding road, and I had to laugh: Millie had passed the Rolls.

Ted drove resolutely, doing his best to ignore his wife, but the two women, hats in hand, had finally caught on and they waved her on. Millie had succeeded in taking the ball away from her beloved, and I found myself pounding my handlebars and shouting, "Way to go, Millie," though of course I was drowned out by the roar of my own Harley.

The parking lots at the top of Moran State Park were beginning to fill up, but I managed to find a decent parking spot right off, at a convenient distance to the parked Rolls. With its decorative conchos hacked off, Millie's bike looked bedraggled and blotchy, like a newly clipped poodle.

Neither of the McCalls was to be seen, nor any of their guests, which meant they were either in the primitive park restrooms or already on the hiking trail up to the observation area. Once off the bike, my squishy ankle turned on me and I went down flat on my face. A bevy of middle aged women of the Rec Equipment school of hiking, the elite of the rugged here in the Pacific Northwest, these hardy hikers came to the rescue, propping me up on my feet, brushing me off as if I were five again and being readied for the church pew by a gaggle of my sisters. I was totally humiliated.

"You heading up the trail on that?" The butch-est of them eyed my ace bandage, thick as the bark on some Doug fir.

"Thought I might."

"Might think again." She wiped the neck of her canteen on her shirttail and passed it to me. I was parched, so I thanked her like a decent guy and took a healthy swig of some cloying sports drink.

"The viewing platform is a good twenty minutes up that narrow trail," Butch said, "if a body is in shape."

"Yes ma'am, I thank you, and have a great day." I took one step on my fat leg and did my best to wipe the grimace off my face. My leg refused to move.

"Here you go, fella." A petite gal in the group weighed down by a heavy backpack handed me a forked limb off some burly madrona tree, and I was startled that it tucked right under my arm.

"I was going to lug that home for granddad, but it's getting heavier by the minute. Take it; you'll be doing me a favor."

"Thank you and God bless," I said. Like a fool, I hobbled on up the trail, doing a nice job of keeping weight off, but my ungrateful limb was screaming by the time I reached the top. I headed for the low stone wall around the lookout and plunked myself down and took a minute or two to collect my wits. I watched a mid-afternoon sun turn the seascape a molten gold, and the tourists were oohing and ahhhing and shutters were snapping, but when I looked around for the McCalls and their guests, I realized that none of them were looking out over the islands.

From behind me came cries of "Mil-lie, Mil-lie," in a clapping and chanting rhythm, and I twisted clear around and found myself staring at Ted McCall's party. Now that I had a better look at the two women along for the ride, I realized they were young things, probably starlets looking for breaks. The swarthy male passenger was in his fifties. He had that foxy sort of face that Warren Beatty made famous, except he was too paunchy to be babe bait, and his mane of hair was steel gray, but he was obviously a sugar daddy type, superbly tanned and dressed in the sportswear that only sports would wear.

Millie's motorcycle jacket was in a heap at their feet. Millie herself had pulled the skirt of her nightgown into a belt made from a piece of what was then the newest thing in gear--bungee cord--turning her nightgown into a bulky set of ad hoc bloomers. She made her way up the side of the stone tower, not by the steps inside the tower that observers were supposed to take, but by the rusting pegs outside that the maintenance people used. I cringed. Maintenance people wore harnesses when they went up there, for the simple reason that this tower was a relic and the pegs were rusting out.

I sat on the stone wall staring in horrified fascination as Millie climbed that tower with a simian grace. At the top, she swung her legs over the rail and took a bow.

I looked around, expecting the park rangers to drag her off there any minute, but none of them were to be seen. The tourists were beginning to thread their way down the trail. A fine afternoon was in progress, a scorching day, time for leisurely dips in the chill mountain lakes.

"Mind if I join you?" a voice said.

"Please," I replied, paying no attention at all to my new companion. I could not take my eyes off Millie, strutting tiptoe around on the top of the tower in a mock high wire act.

"Jim Hardin, aren't you?"

"Halprin." My head snapped around then, and I found myself staring into a set of deep and very weary dark eyes, squinting out at me from beneath a pair of thick but well-pruned brows.

"Mr. McCall." I shifted toward him, attempted to stand.

"Ted. No, don't get up. I'm sorry about your injury."

"Millie," I stuttered. "Things sort of spiraled out of control."

"You beat off some thugs that were after her bike."

"You heard about that?"

"I've heard of nothing else this entire day."

"Then I don't have to…"

"Explain?" He lifted his open palms, a gesture of cease and desist. He had big bony hands, outsized hands for a man of his lanky build.

He pulled off his straw hat and turned it in his hands, while I studied him out of the corner of my eye. He had a thick curly mop of wiry black hair, which I envied, a forehead that was so straight it appeared to have been set with a level, and a graceful long swoop of a nose so perfect it was disgusting. His bony face featured a gash of cheekbone that seemed to work out some painful inner thought before he finally spoke.

"My wife ran amok? I've heard it all before."

"So what can I do for you?"

"I need to get Francis Cordova and his playmates down to the mansion."

"Cordova?"

"Yes. He's a movie guy. These Hollywood types have short attention spans. He'll be bored with Millie's antics in about ten minutes. What I need is for you to persuade Millie to come down from that tower."

"I'll do my best but…"

"But nothing." McCall's eyes bored into mine. "What might look like fun and games to you is business."

"Of course." Said with the best rendition of hearty sincerity I could muster, hiding what I thought: *monkey business.*

"Millie begged me to buy the Rosario estate. The mansion is very run down, you know. She was convinced that restoring the place would help her focus her energies. I indulged her because the property comes with thousands of acres suitable for recreational development."

"I'm aware of that," I said.

McCall raised his eyebrows, looked askance at me.

"One of my friends, Ben Bridges, does real estate. Ben put in a bid for the property at the foreclosure auction."

"Is that so?"

"Ben said you outbid him by a measly five grand."

McCall chuckled. "I had my broker write an offer of five thousand dollars over the next highest bid. That way I didn't make any wild guess at how to top the other offers."

"Excellent." Of course McCall had the deep assets to make such an offer possible. If I learned nothing other than to avoid any full moon poker nights, it was this trick that Ted McCall tipped me to that saved me when I was forced to drop out of college and paint houses for a living. It's how I eventually acquired eighteen fixer uppers, mostly bought out of foreclosure auctions. I had acquired a string of rental properties worth close to a million bucks by the time I turned thirty five.

McCall looked around. "I like you, kid. I'm trusting you with my wife. Despite this… ah… condition of hers, I love her dearly. We found each other right here on this island, you know."

"At the Blysdale house?"

"So she told you?"

"She hinted as much." *As she sat nude at an out-of-tune piano singing moony tunes into a night filled with the warbles of loons.*

Ted McCall glanced at his Rolex as I glanced at him, studying the swag of his moustache draped over a thin upper lip, while artfully emphasizing the ample lower one. I envied his polish and the skills of his Hollywood barber.

"My wife is determined to steal my thunder, but this time Millie has outsmarted herself. Cordova's got a promising film on his hands, where the funding is screwed. He wants me to finance the last few million, offering outrageous interest. I'm dickering for a piece of the action. Word in Hollywood is, this film is hot, hot, hot. I strike a deal with Cordova and make the cash I need to bail us out. Millie is already three times budget on the restoration." McCall clapped me on the arm. "I need you to keep an eye on Millie for the night. She goes into these ecstatic moods, which are followed by the most terrifying bouts of depression. Usually our housekeeper sits with her by the hour, but tonight she has her hands full with our guests."

"Wads?"

"Millie told you?"

"I heard Millie on the phone, pleading with Wads to think well of her."

"A good sign," McCall said. "That means her mania hasn't completely destroyed her better senses. Maybe you can use that some way to get her down from that tower. If you can't do that, you must promise me you'll stick with her, even if it takes all night."

"Of course I'll stay with her. I'll get her down if I have to call in the rescue chopper."

McCall rolled his eyes. "Millie and her chopper."

"The chopper is hers?"

"It might as well be. I had to lease it back from the fire

department or the chief said there was no way he could afford to keep Millie out of trouble." Ted rose. He was on the lean side, slope shouldered, slightly stooped. "Do what you have to do. I'll make it worth your while, very much worth your while." With that, McCall rounded up Millie's audience and made off down the trail with them. As they disappeared, my spirits plummeted.

I had hoped that Millie would notice that she was alone and was losing her audience, but she was in some other world, twirling around in a ballerina number. As so many well brought up little girls, Millie had obviously had some lessons. I stared at the horizon. The sun was in mid arc, giving me ample time and it's a good thing because Millie attracted a new audience, and then another. I figured I'd have a better chance if I could wait for her to exhaust herself and my leg hurt too much to move, so I popped one of the sample pain pills Doc Crock had given me for emergencies, rolled up my Harley jacket and dozed.

By the time I awakened, the shadows had lengthened and the setting sun cast a coppery sheen across the still waters of the sound. I figured we had less then forty minutes to ride down the twisting mountainside highway on our Harleys, and I was not about to try it with Millie in pitch dark. Suppose she went off the road? It would be hell to find the wreckage.

I gave myself ten minutes to try to talk her down. If that didn't work, I had to break into the call box in the tower or have the ranger in charge put out a radio call for the chopper, if I could manage to find the ranger in charge, that is.

"Millie, come on, your guests have gone on ahead. Ted sends his love. He needs you to help entertain your friends." This plea got Millie's attention. She stopped her prancing, took that ballet position, I forget what you call it, where the ladies put their heels together and their toes out. She swept her arm across her body and laughed.

"Oh, right. He never even noticed me."

"Yes, he did, Millie. Ted loves you. Now come on, don't be so hard on the guy. We won't want to run this mountain road after dark."

"Dark? What do you mean? The road will be a silver trail, sooooo fantastic." She blew me a kiss. "You'll just love it, Jim. Wait till I show you."

I was appalled. I featured Millie roaring down a half- lit road like a demon. That did it. So much for reasoning with her. I headed around the side of the stone tower, which stood on a platform with a small entry room to the staircase. The door was padlocked. A sign said the staircase was under repair. If I had to I could pry the hinges off the door and get to the emergency call box. I was searching around for a rock big enough to smash the lock when who should come whistling up the trail but the missing ranger, a guy I knew, thank God.

"Duff Andrews. Am I glad to see you." I had known Andrews since I'd been forced to cut four cords of wood for him as a part of my probation. It was the summer I turned fourteen and Ben's stepson Andy and I had been caught cadging quarters out of a vending machine on the ferry.

"Hey, Jim, nice to see you, kid. Come to chop some kindling for me?"

Andrews never forgot anything, but once Andy and I did our probation, Duff invited us camping. He knew where all the best fishing holes were in the entire park, and reserved a fine campsite for us. We had a blast. Duff was also an outstanding card player: bridge, poker, panguini, you name it. Duff and Marilyn Andrews were frequent guests at the BakerVue Lodge.

"It's Millie McCall. She's up on the tower. Ted's got his hands full with some business deal and left me to fetch her. I can't talk her down and I can't climb up there and grab her." I slapped my fat leg for emphasis.

Andrews sighed, shaking his head. "That poor woman. Let me go get her." He took an enormous key ring off his belt and found the key for the padlock. I followed him inside and attempted to follow him up the stairwell.

"I thought the stairs were torn out."

"Funding never came through. The parks department is two years behind, as usual."

"Can I help you subdue her?"

Duff stopped on the stairs, turned. "That's not the way to deal with Millie. Don't you worry none, we've been through this routine before. If you are going to be included in any more poker nights, Jim, you'd be better off going outside to see how to handle Mrs. McCall." He winked for emphasis.

"Sure, Duff. I leave it to you." I got out of that dank stone room as fast as could I drag myself on my bulky leg, aching like hell in spite of the tight windings of an elastic bandage that made my femur bulge like a sausage. I'd left my madrona crutch by the door and used it to swing along beside the building as best I could. *More of Millie's poker games? No thank you, Millie McCall. You have cost me my ideal summer job and quite possibly a year at school. Thank you Mrs. McCall, but no thanks.*

I hustled back to the stone ledge, far enough away that I could get the best view of the platform at the top of the tower, and what unfolded before my startled eyes was a side of Duff Andrews that I had heard about but had never seen in action.

Andrews was a bit of an actor, a locally beloved star of many of the musical productions put on by Islanders during the long winter months. Tall, lanky, with a thatch of dark brown hair streaked with silver, rugged, thick-browed features, a killer smile and the trim figure he'd kept in shape via his outdoor lifestyle.

Duff swept his peaked hat from his head and put it over his heart as he approached Millie, a practiced gesture. Where had I seen it? When he was the lead in the island production of *Oklahoma*? Maybe. Duff said something to her that I couldn't hear, but when he raised his arms and Millie stepped into them, I realized what it was, an invitation to dance.

Andrews twirled Millie around the platform, waltzing her toward the door to the stairs. Her laughter floated down to me. I glanced around. The sun was down. I shuffled to my feet as best I could, back aching from the strain of balancing on one leg. I hoped to get down to my Harley before Millie emerged from the tower on the arm of the dashing Duff, but the pair caught up with me before I was halfway down the trail. I stepped aside and tried for a casual pose, resting against an enormous boulder as I heard Millie's giggle as a counterpoint to Duff's rumbling baritone.

They came striding down the trail, Millie waggling her fingers at me as they passed, Duff ignored me. As I struggled to catch up, thinking a pox on them both—how dare Millie slight one so ignobly wounded in her service—but then I realized what Duff's strategy was. He was rushing Millie along before she had a chance to think twice and to invent some other strategy to confound us.

Duff put Millie on her Harley, as if helping her onto the back of some fleet steed. He stood by as she revved the machine to life. She blew Duff a kiss as she sped down the trail. Duff lifted his hat as she swept away, a gesture she probably saw in her rear view mirror. As for me, I'd managed to hobble as far as my own machine. I handed the madrona crutch off to Duff and thanked him profusely.

"Don't mention it, son. Millie is not only manic but crafty when she's like this. We've done our routine before. I figure we'll be doing our tower waltz come the next full moon."

"Great, Duff. You can take my place at the next poker night."

"I'd love to, but Millie's events run long past dawn as you know, and I'm a happily married man. My Marilyn's a doll but she gives me grief over Millie's games; I used to be a regular—won some good money but...I've had to bow out."

The ride down from Mt. Constitution is a thrill no Harley rider should miss. I think of it as skating on wheels. On this trip, however, I was amazed at Millie's expertise and disgusted with myself at my own nervousness. I had to take it easy. This was no time to spin out.

It wasn't until we were back on the Horseshoe Highway that I realized that Ben Bridges had pulled one of his jokes on me.

The vast Rosario property had changed hands several times, usually under unfortunate circumstances, before the McCalls acquired it out of yet another bankruptcy auction.

Ben had failed to mention that the McCalls not only bought the estate but also they had changed the name of the mansion itself. Consequently, if I hadn't been following Millie I would have ridden my Harley right past the turnoff from the Horseshoe Highway.

The massive Rosario Resort sign had been uprooted and replaced with a smaller driftwood sign common to the snootiest private estates on the island. "Foxglove" it read in a flowing script comprised of several shades of foxglove purple. A quarter mile down the road was a purplish gate and guard house, not the sort of thing that we were accustomed to on the island. What to make of this? Was our low key island going Hollywood?

Millie stopped to greet the guard, motioned me to follow her, and we wound down the twisting road to the shoreline. Development of the property had begun decades earlier. Posh resort homes were sprinkled along the roadway, but the hillsides were blanketed in masses of the foxgloves that grow profusely on the island, enhanced with the cultivated variety, or so I suspected. I had to admit that Millie's re-name was apt; nevertheless, I was shocked by the paint job. The dignified Rosario mansion had been kept a spanking white for decades. It was now magenta, the color of the darkest of the foxglove flowers. On a mansion the size of a destroyer, this was startlingly New Age. A line of ships' style globes that adorned the façade had been outfitted with daisy yellow sconces. The inner trim of the rounded windows on the main floor were painted a dark green, giving the staid old place the aura of a Mexican bar.

The simple entrance had been gussied up with a long green awning for cars to drive under, very Beverly Hills. Not a bad idea if your main transportation was a Rolls convertible. It does rain a bit here in the San Juans, though the rugged Robert Moran who built the place would have been horrified by anything as pretentious as an awning, or so I suspected.

The Rolls was parked in front of the massive double doors with their nautical hinges and brass fittings. At least the doors hadn't been replaced. A lanky figure in a captain's cap and a white uniform rushed over to help Millie off her Harley and through the front door. I sat outside on my Harley, lingering behind, hoping that Millie would be forgiven by her husband and her housekeeper and that I'd be free to leave.

"Mr. Halprin, nice to see you again," the doorman drawled as he returned, a crutch in hand.

"Such service," I said with a laugh as I took a second look at the narrow, beaky face sheltered beneath the bill of a cap so encrusted with gewgaws that it belonged on a Navy admiral.

"Bones? Is that you?" He clicked his heels and presented the crutch as if it were a flag staff.

"I didn't recognize you under that hat, Bones. Good to see you, man." I slapped him on the back as we shook hands. Bones, aka Eddie Zellwin, was one of Ben Bridges' reclamation projects, Ben being a one-person social service agency, as a great many islanders knew.

"So what do you think of Foxglove?" Eddie said.

"Quite a change of style," I said, adopting a neutral tone.

"Round the island some people don't take to the Foxglove name," Charlie murmured. "Down there to the Pit Stop, some of them call it McMansion."

I had to laugh. "That doesn't surprise me. Islanders prefer to stick with tradition."

"That's where Miz McCall has the last laugh," Bones murmured. "When the mansion was first built, it was maroon."

"Really?"

"It's a matter of record, Mrs. McCall tells me. She thinks Mr. Moran used anti fouling paint, what they applied to the bottoms of ships. Mr. Moran was nothing if not practical, you see."

One of the massive doors opened a crack. Millie poked her head around. "Jim? Where are you? Come on. Wads is waiting. She wants to meet you."

"Yes, ma'am." I tossed off a mock salute. Eddie steadied the bike for me. He handed me the crutch for support as I swung my fat leg over the back of the bike.

"You've thought of everything, Bones."

"Mr. McCall thought it might come in handy." The crutch, an old metal one, was too short. Eddie took it back and pushed some buttons at the bottom of it, drawing it out full length. "A fine thing you done, bringing Miz Millie down off that tower." He handed the crutch back to me.

"Wasn't my doing. It was…"

"You go on now, Mr. Halprin, sir. You're the man, an honored guest." Bones stared up at me, black eyes narrowed in a squint. He squeezed my arm and said nothing more, but in his intense stare, I read a warning.

Once through the door, the old Rosario still reigned. Except for some different artwork, the McCalls had left intact the acres of burnished mahogany paneling, the boaty brass fixtures and the chandelier on chains, designed to swing with the tides. An enormous gallery ran the length of the main floor, furnished with sturdy wood-frame seating that appeared to have been built to stay put on a heaving deck. Millie ushered me to one of these, where she had gone to the trouble to set up a hassock. She ordered me to sit and elevate my leg—a relief, I admit.

A very tall woman soon appeared. She had the square shoulders of a combat veteran, a jawline to match, and a mound of brass-colored hair lacquered into a helmet. She was dressed in a black gown. Her stiletto heels looked as if they could be deployed in combat.

"Stella Wadsworth, you must meet my friend Jim Halprin," Millie gushed. "He saved my day twice over."

"We are all so relieved that you came to Mrs. McCall's rescue, Mr. Halprin." She treated me to a full on smile, revealing a softer side to the crusty Wads.

"Ms. Wadsworth." I struggled to stand but Wads, as she insisted I call her, was having none of it, and she exuded a sort of motherliness where Millie was concerned, inviting her to babble on: "Wait until you hear what transpired, Wads. Young thugs, beaten off by my friend Jim, here. He tore up his leg rushing after me. We were forced to take shelter in the Blysdale house. Poor Jimmy Blysdale. He drowned in the old quarry, you know. Who should appear but our hero, Andy Sullivan in the chopper. Then Ted arrives in the Rolls with his Hollywood set, and what do they want to see? Millie on her Harley…Millie climb the tower on top of Mt…."

Wads broke in: "You must be famished, Mrs. McCall. Let me bring you both some of Chef's salmon chowder."

"Did you say our starlets are at the pool?" Millie said. "I'll do a lap or two. I need to work up an appetite." She dashed off, without a word, leaving me stranded with the housekeeper.

"Mr. McCall extends his welcome," Wads said. "He's in a business meeting at the moment and can't be disturbed. I'll show you to your room. I expect you'll want to, ah, ah…"

"Clean up?"

"Mrs. McCall can be a bit of a…"

"Handful?" Wads acknowledged as much with a sidelong glance. "Mr. McCall was delighted to hear that you managed to get Mrs. McCall safely down from the tower."

"It wasn't me, really. It was…"

"It was amazing," Wads said. "I've suggested to Mr. McCall that he ought to have that tower demolished."

"That might be difficult." *Tear down the observation tower? The most popular attraction in Moran State Park?"*

"It's a safety hazard," Wads snapped. Her expression turned brittle. Case closed. Staircase closed. The tower was hazardous to Millie McCall, therefore it should go, and Wads herself appeared ready to glare it to smithereens. I said nothing more as I hobbled along with her to the elevator beside the main staircase. I didn't dare. Once inside the elevator Wads pushed the button for the third floor, her tone softened and she turned reflective. "Down from the tower is one thing; now's the harder thing for dear Millie, how to come down safely from her own, ah…exuberance."

"She told me, about her…about her…imbalance."

As we stepped out of the elevator, Bones was waiting in the hall with a wheelchair. "Mr. Zellwin will look after you this evening," Wads said, handing him a room key. "You will join us for dinner?"

"I'll do my best. If my leg here cooperates."

"I do hope you'll come. Mrs. McCall would be so disappointed. If you wish, Mr. McCall will call Dr. Crocker and fill a prescription to help with the pain."

Bones helped me settle into a stiff old wheelchair that appeared to have been hand-carved to match the wood paneling of the house. Oddly it was equipped with restraints. Charlie rolled me down to the far end of the long hall.

The rooms at Rosario are small and utilitarian with hand-built teak drawers fastened to the floor, as if anticipating a storm surge. Eddie cranked open a window and helped me to an upholstered chair beside the bed. He wrestled me out of my leather chaps and propped my bandaged leg up on a hassock.

"Thanks, man. How long have you been working here?"

"Got hired on for the summer, thanks to Mr. Bridges. He put in a good word for me with Wads. Mr. Bridges knows Wads from way back. It seems Wads once worked as Carla's assistant at the BakerVue Lodge. I'm to tend to the cars, gas up the boats and do whatever else she tells me. I just got done taking the Rolls around for a ride by the gas pump in town. Me in that Rolls with the red leather seats? I took them two Hollywood dolls around with me. They wanted some smokes from the Pit Stop. I show up with them spectacular women in that snazzy coupe, the guys from the road crew was in there and I thought their eyes would pop out of their heads."

"The women went for a swim in the pool downstairs. Too bad I can't join them."

"You ready for skinny dipping?"

I had to laugh. "I'd be willing but my leg isn't."

"Some excuse," Eddie said. "They invited me but I one-upped those ladies."

"How so?"

"I dared them to come with me to the hot tubs over to the Doe Bay Resort."

"Those two girls will give Millie some competition."

Eddie shook his head. "Them Hollywood babes are in for some swim. They ain't careful, Miz Millie will swim them till they drown."

"Not good for Millie, either."

"Not at all. She'll work herself down to nothing. Miz Millie overdoes. Then she gets so tired and depressed her own husband can't bear to see it, so he flees. That leaves Wads and myself to pull her through."

"You've done the routine already?"

"Last full moon, my first week on the job. Some experience that was. Miz Millie feels so fine she won't take her meds. That puts her over the top."

"As well as way down under."

Eddie nodded. "She goes down? We got to keep watch on her round the clock." He held my wrapped leg over a waste basket and cleaned the sand off with a whisk broom. I was wrapped toe to crotch in thick layers of elastic bandage, which I was not to get wet for another 48 hours. Eddie wrapped the bandage in a plastic trash bag and used duct tape to fasten the bag around my upper leg. He retrieved a luggage rack from the closet and pressed it into service as a shower stool then helped me hobble over to it, turned on the water and left me to do the honors. The hot water felt so good I dozed off in the shower. Eddie had to drag me out of there.

"All right, Mr. Jim Halprin, snap to now," he bellowed. "Slacking on the job will never do." He reached over my head, turned off the shower and handed me a bath towel that could double as a bed sheet. "We'll never get you down to dinner at the rate you move."

"Dinner? I think I'll pass."

"And disappoint Miz Millie? She's counting on you, man."

"What about her husband?"

"Mr. McCall and his guest, that Hollywood fella? They've been huddled in the library for hours. Some deal or other is in the making. Wads was ordered to send dinner in to them and that leaves you to fill in with the ladies."

"The starlets will be there?"

"The ladies are all upstairs here dressing for the occasion."

"And me in my leathers?"

"Tonight we dude you out." On the bed Eddie had laid out a couple of pairs of slacks, a white linen shirt, and a cashmere jacket.

"Been to the Exchange?" The Exchange being the island version of a Goodwill store.

"When you stand in for Ted McCall, you got to look the part." Eddie winked, showing me the McCall monogram on the cuffs of the shirt. "You're the man, Mr. Halprin. You got Millie off that tower in one piece," he cackled. "For that Mr. McCall's giving you the shirt off his back."

"But I didn't...It was..."

"Course you got to keep a close eye on the Mrs. She's been flying high coming on twenty-four hours by now. She could cave in the next minute, and that wouldn't look so good to Hollywood, so then we figure a way to trundle Miz McCall off to bed."

"What do I look for?"

"You'll know when you see it."

Once I was dressed, Eddie settled me into the wheelchair. I couldn't get over the restraints.

"You going to tie me in?"

"No need, Mr. Halprin. You'll love getting pushed around, I expect, but I don't know as breaking my back to save your leg is a fair trade."

"It seems fine to me, Eddie."

"That's what I was afraid of."

"Uppity staff these McCalls have." I sped off down the hall, showing Eddie I could pull my own weight, crippled though I was. I stopped in front of the elevator and waited for Eddie to catch up.

"Wait right here. I'll go fetch Miz McCall." Eddie dabbed sweat off his forehead as he swaggered past me, rolling on the edges of his feet as some Texans do, as if he'd just dismounted from a long ride on a fast pony. I wasn't about to be left behind where Millie was concerned. I pushed my wheelchair along at a discreet distance so as not to rush Eddie into a trot. It wouldn't do to have Eddie sweating and panting when we called for Mrs. McCall.

Millie answered Eddie's knock and invited us into a magnificent suite that took up the entire end of the building.

"Will you have a drink, Jim?"

"I'll wait to have one with you." I declined out of deference to Bones, who not only was on duty but also had certain medical issues that precluded the intake of alcohol.

"All right then. I'll be but a minute, and do have a look around." Every wall in the McCall's apartment was hung with art, collections of Japanese prints, modern paintings from the group known as the Northwest School, art glass by the internationally famous Dale Chihuly, whose Pilchuck Glass School was in Stanwood in the Skagit

Valley, gateway to Camano Island, south of our San Juans.

One entire wall was devoted to the fierce carved masks from the North Coast tribes. Another displayed a full scale model of the battleship Nebraska built by the Moran Brothers' shipyards.

Founder Robert Moran was the mayor of Seattle when the city was destroyed by fire in 1889. Moran's capable handling of the disaster won him a second term, and the city helped him underwrite the bonding needed to win the contract to build the Nebraska, launched in 1905.

Just a minute stretched into thirty. It was close to nine p.m. and another very long and lovely evening was picking up traction, or so I realized as I went to one of the windows open on the sound, where the white globe of the full moon was painting a gleaming path over the inky surface of Cascade Bay.

"Lovely isn't it?" Millie trilled as she approached me, bending to kiss me on the cheek as I sat in the wheelchair.

"And so are you, Mrs. McCall," I said, adopting the Ben Bridges method of dealing with the opposite sex. All women are lovely, every one, was his motto, and in Millie's case it was at least half true. Millie's eyes were puffy from lack of sleep and her dark eyes seemed glazed and unfocused. Yet there was no denying her elegance. This was the first time I had seen Millie McCall when she wasn't in a nightgown—except, of course, for my recent exposure to all of her back at the Blysdale house.

"You clean up nicely, Mrs. McCall." Millie possessed a boyish style of beauty, a Mia Farrow type waif but for her thick black/brown hair piled on her head in a sophisticated twist with tendrils falling out over her forehead and trailing down her neck.

She wore a teal gown dropped low on the hip to show off her svelte, fashion model's shape. Her skirt was pleated above the knee, revealing her shapely legs.

She went straight to the window and held her hands up to the moonlight, holding the pose so long that Eddie and I exchanged glances, conveying our mutual consternation.

When she finally turned back to us, her face had lost its slack look and the puffiness was gone; her eyes were glowing, so much so that the hackles prickled the back of my neck and goose bumps shot chills along my forearms.

"Millie Moonbeam," I blurted.

She smiled, the way she always did, with an uplifting of her lips, and not the toothy display we think of as a dazzling smile. Millie's smile was indulgent in a way, a kind of smirk. It said that Millie knew something that the rest of us didn't.

"Are you making fun of me, Jim?"

I laughed off my inadvertent insult. "If I had your way with the moon, Millie, I'd have healed my fat leg already."

"You have every reason to be jealous." She bent to kiss me on the cheek, treating me to a whiff of a very seductive perfume and a close look at her drippy diamond and emerald earrings.

"Let's go, gentlemen." Millie swept toward the door on heels so high that her legs appeared a foot longer than those of the Harley rider in her Doc Martens.

Millie propped aside the massive bedroom door with its ship's hinges while Eddie maneuvered my wheelchair out, taking care that my extended leg wouldn't get bashed as I rode across the sill. I took over my own locomotion. That left Eddie to escort Mrs. McCall to the elevator and push the button to the first floor.

We emerged into the lower lobby in fine style, but without fanfare, since the guests had already assembled in the great room. I followed my companions the length of the gallery to a massive room here firelight played on the chipped marble of the fireplace.

Though it was midsummer, the Pacific Northwest nights are still capable of their wonderful chill—very fine sleeping weather—which accounts for the appeal of the San Juan Islands, as hoards of sweltering visitors from the steaming southern deserts of California, Arizona, Nevada, and New Mexico, will attest.

Millie's grand entrance on the arm of Eddie Zellwin went largely unnoticed, however. The room was empty but for the two starlets who sat opposite Pepper Flanigan, the island's most entertaining musician. To his credit, when he saw Millie, he did a fanfare riff, and launched into a few bars of "Moonlight Becomes You."

Eddie had escorted Millie to one of the sofas on either side of the fireplace and I guided my wheelchair to the end of it, so that I could talk to Millie. Eddie fetched champagne for her. On a tip from Eddie, I opted for an Oregon pinot noir so renowned that the output of its cellars goes into private hands before it ever appears on the market.

Wads, who had been supervising a buffet setup, rushed over to greet Millie, gushing about her lovely gown.

"I'm starved, Wads," Millie said. "What is keeping the men?"

"Mr. Ted sent his apologies, ma'am. He's had a tray sent up for himself and Mr. Cordova. It seems they are busy with some business negotiation. They expect to be joining you ladies for brandy and coffee prior to the screening."

"Well," Millie huffed. "I wish I'd known. I'd not have bothered to get dolled up. These earrings are killing my ears and I hate this damned panty hose. My starlet friends and I would have been just as happy to sit around in our jammies."

"What? No red nightgowns?" I now account for this blunder by the fact that I'd belted down my first pinot in a bit of a hurry and was already halfway through my second; if I didn't slow my big mouth down, the end of my evening was certain to be strictly noir.

Millie stared at me. Here I was committing some gaffe every fifteen minutes.

"No offense, Millie. I just happen to love ladies in red." I applied my most earnest tone and Millie laughed.

"I ought to smack you Jim, but you are forgiven."

Flanigan broke for the second set. Eddie seated Millie at a table for four near the buffet. I wheeled along and Eddie removed a chair to put me opposite Mrs. McCall. The two starlets rushed over to embrace Millie. The dark haired one, Tina Guillette, made Millie promise to take her out on a midnight ride on her Harley. The blonde, Rita Tabore, wanted to go hiking at dawn with Millie on the bluffs overlooking the estate.

I kept my mouth shut long enough to learn that the two young women were graduates of the Cornish School of the Arts in Seattle. Tina was a Washington State girl who grew up on an apple orchard in Wenatchee. Rita was a Hollywood kid, the daughter of a highly paid cameraman who had shot famous films for the biggest directors in Hollywood. Both of them were signed with an agent who worked for Mr. Cordova, who in turn co-produced films for half a dozen studios.

After dinner, Rita and Tina did a song and dance medley of show tunes, which they had done for their graduation project from Cornish. At one point I overheard them confiding to Millie that they had wangled the trip up to the islands so that Tina could visit her family. She had dragged Rita along the better to avoid any entanglements with Cordova, a man who already had several ex-wives and a reputation for extracting sexual favors from starlets.

At the end of the act, to wild applause from Eddie, Wads, and myself, the girls invited Millie to join them for an encore. Mrs. McCall kicked off her shoes and launched into a wild and very athletic dance that she seemed to have invented on the spot.

At that point Ted McCall arrived with Mr. Cordova, who cheered Millie on. When she got back to the table, Cordova offered to do a screen test for Millie. She thanked him coyly, downplaying the idea, but I could tell she was flattered.

"Ask her about her career as a stunt woman," Ted McCall quipped.

Pepper Flanigan came back for a second set, a medley of moony tunes: "Don't Shoot the Moon," " Shine on Harvest Moon," "Mr. Sun, Mr. Moon," "Dancin' in the Moonlight," "Moon of Love," "By the Light of the Silvery Moon," and "Mr. Magic Moon." I'd never have known all the titles, except that Flanigan, aka, the Dean Martin of the San Juans, crooned a few bars of each tune. When he got to "Moonlight Bay," the McCalls got up to dance and Mr. Cordova swept Rita to the floor, whereupon Eddie magically appeared to partner Tina.

I was drowsy from the excellent meal: Olympia oysters, fresh salmon right from the sound, filet mignon, Alaska king crab, and all the trimmings. I was fading by the minute but determined to stay awake for the private screening of the movie for the evening. While the party cranked away on the dance floor, I rolled out to the deck to inhale some sea-and-pine scented oxygen, hoping to clear my head, but wound up witnessing a skirmish between the McCalls instead.

Had I dozed off? I can't say. There was Millie, arms upraised, receiving another charge from the moonlight, and I kept quiet in the shadows, not wanting to startle her, but her husband felt no such compunction when he arrived.

"Millie dear, what are you doing out here?" he said as he arrived on the deck, closing the door behind him. "You have guests, remember?" He stepped in close behind her, slipping his arms around her waist, nuzzling her neck.

"Cordova wants to do a screen test," Millie said, arms still upraised, swaying now, like a siren.

"He would," Ted said. "He has a thing for beautiful women."

"My own road picture starring Millie McCall."

"Mrs. McCall in her nightgown, speeding over mountain terrain on her flashy Harley?" Ted hooted. "Come on Millie, you don't want that."

Millie dropped her arms, spun around and pushed Ted away. "You mean you don't want that."

"Making a movie is a grueling endeavor," Ted said. "I've been on these stage sets. They do scenes over and over, ten, twelve hours at a time. That kind of thing could kill you, Millie." Ted gently pulled her arms down, crossing them across her chest, and I was stuck. I took care not to let them know I was taking in this private moment.

Millie closed her eyes, resting her head against her husband's chest. "It wouldn't do to try to sleep," she said. "I can't calm myself when I'm feeling so wonderful, so privileged."

Ted sighed. "You're off your meds, Millie."

"I took them this morning."

"Like hell you did." He released her and turned her toward him, still cradling her in his arms. She stared at the floor. He took her chin in one hand. "Look at me, Millie. I'm your husband. I love you. But when you start this baying at the moon, I can tell."

"I'm not baying at the moon."

"Okay, so whatever you call it. Moon worship?"

"I took my meds. I remember."

"This morning you had to be rescued by chopper from the Blysdale house, Millie. I don't have to remind you what this costs us."

"Was that this morning?"

"You see? You don't know; you have no clue whether or not you took you meds. Please, Millie, I don't know how many more times you go over the top before you come to serious harm."

It was well after dark, close to ten p.m. before the party trundled upstairs to the theatre, a handful of us, including staffers Eddie Zellwin and Wads, a very small audience in a room that could seat forty.

Musician Pepper Flanigan did the honors, welcoming the guests. It was a way for Ted McCall to lay claim to bragging rights, I suppose. Flanigan narrated a short film clip about the founder of Rosario, Robert Moran and his Irish clan. The stress of rescuing Seattle after the fire and launching the Nebraska within the space of a few years was ruinous to Moran's health. Under doctors' orders to retire, Moran built the mansion, using concrete construction, a foundation that extends 20 feet underground..."

I viewed this history through the ironic voice of Ben Bridges. He figured that Moran ordered more materials than needed for a battleship and that the mansion was built cost plus, at government expense, but you have to realize, Ben is a bit of a cynic.

The movie screen dropped down over the surrounding pipes of Moran's pride and joy, a magnificent pipe organ with close to two thousand pipes. Flanigan excused himself and exited via a small door nearly invisible in the exquisite paneling. He next appeared overhead, on a balcony at the side of the room, which formed the organ loft.

To demonstrate the power of the organ, Flanigan played a snippet of *The Phantom of the Opera,* while the movie appeared overhead, the Phantom fleeing from a torch-bearing mob intent on lynching him.

Ted McCall had seated me on the aisle, next to Millie. He kept a protective hand clamped over his wife's arm. Millie's body trembled with excitement as she watched the scene.

"Sweetheart, would you please calm down?" he said.

Flanigan came to the balcony and explained that Rosario had one of the first home theaters in the nation, and now thanks to the pioneering work of McCall Optics, the re-christened Foxglove had the finest theater projectors in the country.

This remark caught my attention. So? This was why Ted McCall spent most of his time in Hollywood? He wanted to sell movie projectors?

"Did you make the deal?" Millie whispered.

"Later," Ted murmured, stroking her arm.

Lights came up briefly. Flanigan announced that tonight's fare, a screening of what would soon to be a Hollywood classic, *Thelma and Louise*, would prove to be an historic first screening for the Foxglove mansion.

Flanigan introduced Cordova as a co-producer of the film. "That's a stretch," Cordova said as he got up in front of his audience, the handful of us present applauding loudly. I filled my lungs and blasted the room with my shriek of a whistle, a trick I had learned from my grand orator of a father whose lung power could command a hall without the use of a microphone. I banged the back of my good leg, the booted one, on the frame of my wheelchair for good measure.

"Every actress in Hollywood was after a part," Cordova said. The cross-country odyssey of the two women, Thelma and Louise, is a reversal of the standard road picture, of males on the lam. Several famous producers wanted to make the picture, but they couldn't get the right director.

"What is less well known—and why I am here tonight—is that there is a financial snafu attached to this magnificent film. Funding has gone awry. Our European financier has not delivered as promised. What you are seeing tonight is one of the few copies of the film in existence, which I'm allowed to show only to prospective backers.

"Our director is beside himself. We've had to push back the release date and we can't do that more than once. Our co-producer, this very charming Italian fellow, is not answering the phone. The bank that was supposed to be paying out the last few million claims to know nothing about it, and that my friends, is where we are." Cordova signaled his frustration with raised open palms.

"I've appealed to my dear friend Ted McCall here, who stands to make a fortune for us all by supplying funding we need so desperately to keep from derailing what everyone in the industry believes is a surefire hit. Without further blather from me, I want you to be among the first people in the nation to view this breathtaking spectacle." Cordova turned to the balcony. "Ready, Mr. Flanigan?"

As the lights dimmed, Mr. Cordova introduced his latest young starlets, Tina and Rita. "One of these days I expect we'll be making a film about a beautiful dancer and her Harley Davidsons and our very own Millie McCall, a unique character, as the inspiration for a feature film."

We all stood up and applauded, the few of us who witnessed this tribute to Millie, who stood mute, tears in her eyes. She leaned into Ted's shoulder. He ruffled her hair and kissed the top of her head.

The movie started. It was wildly popular with Millie and the two starlets, but not my thing. With nine genteel sisters, I just couldn't feature any one of them murdering anyone, even if the dude was a rapist who deserved it, and so I confess I sort of dozed through most of the film. I was startled awake by a loud banging.

Thelma and Louise had gotten the better of a traffic cop who tried to arrest them. They had locked the cop in the trunk of his car. A Jamaican Rasta boy who for some reason happens to be bicycling along the road, and this is in Moab, Utah, well, this Rasta dude hears the commotion, the cop hammering at the underside of the trunk lid he's trapped in. The Rasta takes a drag off his ganja cigarette and blows it into a bullet hole in the trunk. That scene I loved, and I bellowed out my appreciation, turning heads in the audience, much to my embarrassment.

Suddenly Millie yanked out of Ted's arms. She formed a chorus with Rita and Tina. The three of them were doing some sort of very wild dance front and center, right beneath the movie screen, the two starlets mimicking Millie's moves, which were jerky and primitive. Millie went into a spin, her arms flailing like wheels in gear, a reprise of the same moves we had earlier seen. Her frenzied steps gave me a very bad case of heartburn, probably brought on by my indulgence in the pinot noir, but who knows? I didn't like this performance one bit, and Ted McCall hated it. He slid to Millie's seat beside me and put his mouth to my ear.

"Jim, my man, we are out of time. We have to rein Millie in. I've seen this finale of hers dozens of times. She's going to crash any minute."

"What do we do?"

"I've sent Wads down to bolt the outer doors, so she can't take off on her Harley. Eddie Zellwin is posted in the hall, right in front of the elevator in case Millie dodges past us. I want you to block the screening room exit with your wheelchair. The movie has a few minutes to run. When the lights come up I'll sweep Millie up in my arms and carry her out of here, making it look like a seduction. Nobody has to know my poor darling is headed for a padded room and restraints."

On the screen, the law had caught up with Thelma and Louise. Lights and sirens blared as they made straight for the Grand Canyon in their green T-Bird convertible. I rolled to the back of the room and parked my chair in front of the door. I could see that Millie, as she came out of her dance, was looking for a way to escape. I swept my arms wide, forming a welcoming embrace. Millie veered toward me and I thought she'd come straight for me and I could lock her in my arms, but as she passed the small door to the organ loft, she turned around and went back. She yanked the door open and disappeared up the inside stairs.

"Millie," Ted shouted, racing after her but the door slammed in his face. He tried the lock. It was bolted from the inside. Ted shouted for Pepper Flanigan, but there was no answer. We were later to learn that Flanigan had gone out for a smoke on the tiny balcony, where

Robert Moran liked to linger while his employees down below thought they were hearing the great man playing the organ; instead, what they were hearing was a player organ. Flanigan couldn't hear us over the movie sound blasting from the balcony.

On the screen the two women, Thelma and Louise, were in their parrot green T-Bird; the camera closed in on their faces. Millie appeared, hovering over the balcony, arms upraised, her face serene, and I shall never forget her elegant ballerina's pose, the blissful expression on her face, and her hands signaling that the final action is about to begin.

On the screen, Thelma says to Louise, "Something's crossed over in me. I can't go back..."

Millie's face glowed, her serenity sent chills coursing through my body. I am convinced that Millie McCall had assumed a state of grace, that something had crossed over in her, but I was terrified.

"Ted, she's on the balcony," I shouted, racing the wheelchair down the side aisle. Ted couldn't hear me and was battering the door to the loft with his fists.

On the screen, Thelma and Louise race toward the canyon. Ahead of them lies their only escape.

Thelma: "Let's keep going."

Louise: "You sure?"

Louise kissed Thelma hard on the mouth. Arms extended, Millie soared over the balcony as the T-Bird flew into space and the action stopped mid-air, leaving Thelma and Louise in their T-Bird, forever in flight.

Even though I am a believer and I saw with my own eyes that Millie McCall had seized her freedom, it wounds my heart to this day that I was not in time to break her tragic fall. To this day, it wounds me to think that the exuberant Millie McCall never again rode out on her Harley on the night of the full moon. To this day, whenever I return to my beloved San Juan Islands, someone is apt to recall that I was the last man to leave Millie McCall's final poker night, and a hush will fall over the room.

OUT ON A LIMB

I rode with the swaying branch of a maple, knees bent, arm lifting like a wing. I was a hawk, talons clamped on a breezy perch, the wind ruffling my feathers. I was balanced on a brawny limb about halfway up an enormous tree. I was nearly level with the second story deck of the Ritter house, a sprawling cedar manse I much admired. Below in the distance, the stately firs on the hillside dived into the mirror of the tidal lagoon at Doe Harbor.

After the freshet passed, I shifted position. I clamped my pincer of a hand to a branch overhead and used my free hand to loop a flip line over the branch above my head, snugged it around the tree trunk and snapped the end of it into my saddle. I was about to saw off a branch at eye level when my concentration was broken by a slap of a screen door and a rushing of footsteps. From the deck below and behind me came a sharp intake of breath.

"You all right?"

"Yes, ma'am." There was no swinging round in the saddle to acknowledge the lady of the house; I'm not into foolhardy moves. I might think like a bird, might sit on a branch like one, but I recognize my limitations by now and I bear wounds to prove it. I was tethered to one of the strongest branches on the tree and wore steel stirrups with sharp prongs that allow me to walk right up a tree trunk if need be. I waggled one of my steel core lines as a means of saying hello and tapped the branch with my saw.

"If I prune this one, you'll get a better view of the sound and the islands in the distance, but not the fire station in the foreground."

"Oh?"

"That's my take on it, ma'am. Charlie thought I should take the branch I'm standing on, but it screens out the house below you. My thought is, you want to create the illusion that there's nothing here but just the family hidden in their tree house above the mirror of the lagoon."

"Ah." I heard her footsteps as she walked this way and that, checking out the view. I was glad to have her input. I love my work; it's like sculpting nature in a way, but a second opinion from the client is the way to get more jobs, and Charlie Ritter couldn't stay on to supervise.

While the lady made up her mind, I sat back in my saddle and loosened my hard hat enough to let a breeze chill my sweaty skull and slather my face. Call it a maple-scented aftershave.

"Okay, I see what you mean," she finally said. "Go ahead. Take that branch."

A few swift strokes of my hand saw, curved like a scimitar, did the deed. I holstered my saw and swung the heavy branch out and away, so that it wouldn't tangle in the branches below me as it fell to the ground, but even so, the whole tree shuddered as the limb bounced from one descending branch to the next as it spiraled to the ground.

"How's that?" I said to the feminine voice; "Check the view, would you, Sheila? Let's see what else needs to be done."

Sheila Ritter took her time in these matters. She moved along the deck, checking the view from all angles. I removed my goggles to wipe the sweat out of my eyes, and happened to glance around in the direction of the footsteps. I was met at eye level by a pair of stems lithe as two of the alder trunks standing in the grove downhill from the maple. I couldn't help but admire those limbs, clad as they were by jeans tight as bark. My eyes swept the top of a trim frame. This was not Mrs. Shiela Ritter I was talking to, but some budding edition of that grand lady.

"Pardon me," I said. "I thought I was talking to Mrs. Sheila. You must be Mrs. Ritter's..."

"Niece," she said, "I'm Willow Ritter." She had her aunt's oval face and high forehead and that long nose that was a tad long and that chin that was a tad short, and somehow it was a fine combination.

"Willow?" I said. "A wonderful name."

63

She laughed, showing very straight, very white teeth, and tossed her head, setting her long hair to rippling. Sable brown her hair was, light and silky in texture and it shone the way wet bark does as it dries in the afternoon sun.

"Willow suits you."

She made a wry face as she tucked one hand into the back pocket of her jeans. "My friends call me Will—as in Willful." She leaned on the deck rail.

"Better than Stub as in Stubborn," I saluted her with a wave of my scimitar. "I'm Gabriel Steed. My friends call me Gabe on account of I'm neither willful nor stubborn."

"Really?" she said. "Then why did Uncle Charlie send me to keep an eye on you? He said you might decide to chain yourself to our maple."

"Your uncle and I have some history."

"So you are a tree hugger then?"

"Let's just say I'm a tree admirer."

"We need more of those." Her tone was on the tart side, but a flash of white teeth suggested she was teasing.

"I'll agree with you there." I holstered the saw in my tool belt and donned my goggles. I'd have enjoyed talking to Willow some more. One of the few drawbacks to my occupation is that there's not so much feminine company to be found out in the woods. However, the Ritter job was one of the toughest of my day, which was why I tackled it first, but even so I ran late that day; I have to admit, because I took care to please Willow Ritter.

We took out some pencil thin pines that were being stunted by their healthier cousins to open up the view from the deck to the south; we topped the alder grove rather than fell the trees, since they hid the neighbor's house and garage. Alder used to be considered a trash tree, I told Willow, but alder pulls toxicity out of the ground. In Russia, they plant alders in garbage dumps to purify the air, a passing remark that impressed Miss Ritter.

"You talk like someone with a degree in…"

"Arboreal science," I said.

"Where did you go to college?"

"The Northwest Arboreal Institute," I said. "I'm working on my master's." In how to bullshit attractive women. "And yourself?"

"University of Washington, marine biology." As she leaned out over the deck, the morning sun washed over her hair, bringing out a touch of red in it. Madrona red it was, kiln dried.

"You following the orca whale pods?"

She nodded, shading the sun out of her eyes with a long-fingered hand. She had thick, straight eyebrows that converged tightly on the base of her shapely nose. Was it the brows or her character that gave her face such intensity? And why should any such notion concern me?

"Did Uncle Charlie tell you?" She crossed her arms, a gesture demanding the whole truth.

"Most of the U-Dub marine biology majors work in my friend Doc Hanrahan's orca whale study."

Willow raked her fingers through her mane, considering this, while I considered her hair, parted at the side in one of those messy-on-purpose parts. Her hair fell forward over her shoulders in raggedy swaths nearly touching her breasts, ample breasts, blooming high on her chest. She wore a pink, long-sleeved tee shirt that covered her hips and her tight belly, tight as a drum and I felt a tug of remorse at needing to move on, to get on with my day, and I cautioned myself to beware of the beautiful Willow. Women, they aren't worth the trouble. Women cramp a lifestyle as fluid as mine happens to be.

I ran into Miss Willow again a few weeks later, on the solstice, June 21, the day of the Solstice Parade. I walked into her, I should say. At the Solstice Parade, I lead every freak, geek, transcendentalist, spirit weaver, shape-shifter, or whatever, parading all these strange types down main street in what's likely the funkiest parade in America.

As head stilt walker, I wear my green heart on my sleeve. My robes are cut from an old army blanket, hand painted with ancient signs and symbols. I wear a garland of cedar boughs twined with wild strawberry vines, white flowers bright as Christmas lights in winter foliage. I carry a pair of Chinese lanterns at either end of my balance pole. I strut along to the solemn TAMB TAMB TAMB TAMB that the solstice drummers prefer.

I heard my name called several times and was busy waving and bowing, so many in the crowd know me by now, but when the slender figure with one hand in her hip pocket stepped into the center of the street and raised her camera, I realized it was Willow

Ritter trying to attract my attention. She snapped my photo on her cell phone camera. I nodded, dipped my head at her, swung clear around and bowed to her while the marchers stepped in place, bowing to everyone. The crowd clapped, hooted, whistled.

We marched the length of Main, and then swung through the farmers' market on the town green and eventually disbanded at the beer garden. Everyone on the island had turned out to hear the local musicians play on the new, hand-lacquered stage. It was a hot day; I stripped off my costume and lashed it into a bedroll, when a tankard from the beer tent appeared beneath my nose.

"Time for Father Earth to chill."

"Willow," I said. "Thank you kindly." She held her own tankard in her other hand, inviting herself to join me and so I unrolled the army blanket and patted a place for her on it. We claimed a patch of lawn in front of the stage where we could watch the concert. The San Juan Islands abound with talented musicians and they were all eager to perform on the new stage.

Stilt walking might look easy but it requires enormous exertion. The stilts are heavy and cumbersome to move in. The whippy balance pole seems to burn in my arms after an hour or three, all of which left my arms numb and my belly ravenous. There's no finer food to be had than at the farmers' market where I bought plates of grilled oysters and smoked ham and havarti cheese sandwiches made from bread baked that morning and served fresh on the green.

The Orcas Symphony took the stage, the name, of course, an island in-joke. For instance, the string section is comprised of several fiddles, a banjo or two, a few guitars and a saw.

The Symphony cranked out its offerings, enhanced by a very professional sound system donated by a world-class studio musician. That's the lavish/funk way things are done here on Orcas Island.

Willow nodded along, sending tremors through her gossamer hair with every move. "Awesome stage," she murmured. "I've never seen anything like it. Funny, but I don't recall seeing it last season."

"It wasn't here," I said. The stage she referred to was a mini forest of lacquered madrona timbers left in their treelike shapes forming a swaying still life along the sides of the band shell.

"The stage was started last fall. The local musicians wanted an open air stage, so somebody got a fund-raiser going, and I was called upon to find the madronas."

"Really?" Her eyes went wide.

"The idea was to take only logs fallen in the winter storms or live trees whose survival was marginal."

"A green stage, then?"

"I suppose you could call it that, but madrona has to go through a long cure before it's useable in construction."

"So how did you find the logs?"

"I get around the woods," I said. "Lots of carvers here need wood. Various owners are glad to harvest their deadfall. Don't tell the tree huggers, but this island is full of deadfall. A lightning strike in a dry season could set a fire that could ruin this whole island."

"Suppose a tree fell over the power line?"

Her question took me aback. I looked Willow in the eye, looked for signs of malice. Brown shot through with hints of green and gold, her eyes were. Brown eyes are tricky. They tend to change color with the light. I sipped my beer while I considered what her Uncle Charlie might have told her about my accident. I took another sip, weighing the context of the conversation. Her expression was still, guileless, her straight brows level, and so I let it pass. Why be defensive? Her uncle was my friend.

"Trees fall on the power line all the time. A hard winter will do it," I said, saluting her with the prosthesis that serves me as my left hand.

The beer kept on flowing and at some point we went down to the Sound View tavern and found a place on the deck. We ate bowls of creamy clam chowder and sides of mussels and sweet potato fries. Willow brought me up to speed on what she'd been doing. When she wasn't assisting Doc Hanrahan in the whale studies, she had side jobs leading kayak tours and working on a cruise boat when she could fit them in. As it happened, she had Monday off and so that's how I came to invite her to come along with me to Waldron, the island where simple living is the key. There's no power at all except by generator, no roads to speak of, and guests are by invitation only.

That night I invited Willow to our solstice vigil down in Deer Harbor, across the lagoon from the Ritter tree house, where the bonfire and the barbeque goes on until the wee hours. If the tide is in, the hardier souls skinny dip in the tidal lagoon by the light of the full moon, if there is one, which there was, a solstice moon.

A white northern night backlit by a moon wrapped in clouds made eerie work of Willow's slender body. She wishboned into the black waters and came up screaming. I dived in to be with her, fool that I am. My arms, wracked with pain from the days' overreaching, cramped in protest. My shins burned from hauling on the heavy stilts. By the time I swam back to the canoe, Willow had shinnied aboard, but I was all in, much to Willow's amusement.

"You're my slave now, Steed," Willow said. Laughing wantonly, she threw me a tow line and paddled me to shore. We stumbled back to my camper rig, rolled ourselves into the army blanket and a sleeping bag, took refuge in each others' arms, and shivered our way into bliss.

Call it a frolic, call it a fantasy. A woman like Willow I didn't need in my life, but our time together was unreal, and it was all because of a lost baby whale from L Pod, L-98, Luna. We were in my Boston Whaler powered with a twenty-five horse Evinrude. We were approaching Waldron Island when this nuisance of an orca whale gave chase and Willow was delighted. She took a million photos of this character, and that was how she came to make the significant identification, the thing nobody thought was possible: that a whale as young as Luna could be lost from his family and survive. At that point, of course, we had no idea that Luna was Luna. He was just a lonely pup out to play. He swam in the wake of the boat and then he surfaced at the bow of our Whaler and he'd nudge the bow where Willow sat and she reached out and patted him and he loved it, you could tell.

This made me nervous. This was a baby orca whale, but he was a whopping baby and when he surfaced I realized he was a sight longer than we were and could easily capsize us. I asked Willow to sit down in the bow and not encourage any more antics.

Willow, being every bit as willful as she said she was, paid no attention, except she did zip up her life jacket. I powered the Evenrude way down while I lashed my gear to the side of the boat. I had everything stuffed into a big canvas duffel. I figured that if this orca flipped the boat my best chance of recovering my stuff would be to lash it to the side of the Whaler.

Fortunately for us we were in one of the most stable crafts afloat because Luna did his best to flip us on his next pass. He nudged up under the bow; Willow lost her balance as the bow stuck its nose in the air. I caught her as she tumbled past me, but even so, the boat was swamped; my duffel was soaked and I said a prayer for my chainsaw in there. Willow lost her little tape recorder over the side, the one where she made notes for her reports, but I was busy bailing out the boat and kept my head down so Miss Will couldn't read on my face certain black thoughts I was having.

Willow took off one of her rubber boots and helped bail. After we cleared the water it took me a good forty minutes and about thirty five pulls to start the outboard.

Willow sat down in the bow and held on tight and closed her eyes while I powered up and did my best to outrun Luna but he followed us to the dock at Waldron where Jerry Gantz, caretaker for my client's property, took the line I tossed. Jerry lobbed a stick into the water and the whale went after it just like a big puppy and I got Willow and my soggy gear out of the Whaler, but my legs were as shaky as my mood.

Jerry, a wizened old logger type, went on about how that orca pup was becoming a problem. Luna took out the prop on the supply boat last week and there were women and children aboard and if that whale capsized the supply boat, the island's link to civilization, if people were put at risk, there was no telling what might become of Luna.

This was, of course, a red flag to Willow and she pumped the old boy for information. Jerry has a ruddy round face wreathed in fine white hair and deep set eyes. His fluffy eyebrows waved in the breeze as he drove us in a battered pickup truck, one of the few vehicles ever to be barged to the island, and he drove us up a logging trail to a campsite where a crew was logging off diseased pines that had been marked for clearing by a forester, clearing and burning the deadfall. I had hours of work to do, but Willow was insistent. She text messaged Doc Hanrahan about finding an orca pup that seemed to be lost from its pod.

Old Jerry was in his glory, ferrying Willow around to talk to the residents on the island and taking their stories of the sightings, trying to document how long the whale pup had been hanging around Waldron.

Come quitting time, Jerry came to get me, but Willow was gone. She was down at Jerry's cabin; she had organized a potluck supper, the sort of thing that people on the island love, a chance to gather around a campfire and swap stories and chow down.

Willow made a pot of chicken stew and biscuits and I have to say I was amazed. I'd figured her for one of those spoiled college kids who lived on trial mix when in the woods. Willow had everybody all excited about this baby orca. By the end of the evening it was too dark to go back to Orcas. I had four clients scheduled for the following day but the first one would not expect me before ten a.m. I like to let the trees dry out before I start in with the trimming; we could leave at dawn and I'd have ample time to make my appointments. Fortunately, I'd managed to get my chainsaw running. No harm done.

Jerry offered us his "guest house," a lean-to with a fire pit and a couple of sleeping bags that smelled like dog. Willow was thrilled with the arrangement. Doc H. was arriving next morning with a crew of students he'd rounded up for the new project. "You won't have to haul me around, Gabe, she said, tucking that hand into her back pocket. "I'll catch a ride back to Orcas with the class."

I was lulled by Jerry's homemade beer—lethal stuff—heavy on the alcohol, and so it wasn't until an hour or two before dawn when I felt a cold draft in the sleeping bag that I realized how grumpy I was.

I hated the fact that Willow wasn't going back to Orcas with me. I hated the idea that Doc Hanrahan was coming to fetch her. Doc had his pick of the female students of the season and I just knew that Willow was certain to be his choice. This mattered not a whit to me; or so I told myself. It was Willow I was looking out for, and I turned it over and over in my mind while she was up rustling about, starting the morning campfire. What could I say to warn her?

Willow handed me a cup of camp coffee, full of grounds, wonderful stuff on a brisk morning.

"I can't stay on to wait for my friend, Doc Hanrahan. Say hello to that old letch for me."

Willow pulled her sleep-rumpled mane from the back of her neoprene jacket. "Not to worry, Steed." She took a big swig of her coffee and wiped away grounds on the back of her hand. "Doc's a known quantity. I can handle myself."

Sure she could. Willow handled herself right out of my life. I neither saw nor heard from her for the next several weeks. Not that I cared. Not at all. No way.

Active as I am, I suppose it was inevitable that I should run into

Willow Ritter again. I was out to Buckhorn Bay Lodge one Sunday morning three or four weeks later and I was trimming trees in the grove around the hot tubs when what should I observe but Miss Willow and Professor Hanrahan taking a tutorial hot tub in a cloud of hot steam. I did my best to ignore their presence but one of the branches I was standing on proved rotten. Damn. How could I not have noticed? I grabbed the branch I was about to trim overhead when my footing went out from under me and my chain saw, swinging by its tether, went sliding down through the branches; the saw landed in a thicket of blackberries that shelters the hot tubs from prying eyes.

Their two heads popped up and Willow rose like a water sprite, and the white stripe across her bare chest went through me like a knife and she grabbed a towel and wrapped herself in it and then she saw it was me.

Damned if she didn't slip into some rubber boots and come stand at the base of the tree, wrapped in the towel. Her hair was matted and her shoulders were dripping and she squinted up at me, sheltering her eyes with one hand so it was hard for me to see the expression on her face.

"You all right, Gabe?"

A grunt was all I could manage. The branch I was hanging from wouldn't bear my weight but I'd managed to hook one leg around the trunk and had spurred a foothold for the other into the tree trunk. I had picked up a mouthful of pitch somewhere and spat it out as I said, "No problem."

"Your face is bleeding."

I wiped the side of my head on the arm clamping the overhead branch. I'd reached the limit of the chain on my safety harness and so I shinnied up a foot or two to relieve the pressure and Doc's voice drifted in my direction. He has the deepest bass I've ever heard and his greeting reached me as I released myself.

"I've got your saw, Gabe."

"Thanks, Doc," I said. Professor H. and I were friends, or used to be. I often stayed at one of his cabins on Buckhorn Bay when I'm working this end of the island, but avoided doing it this time, and I sat there in that tree, still as some squirrel waiting for the hunter to go away, but the two of them just stood there watching me.

"Just put the saw at the base of the tree, if you would." I fetched my scimitar saw off my tool belt and began making silly cuts of small branches.

"Your face is still bleeding," Willow said.

"I'll live." I whacked off branches and let them fall. If they landed on the heads of my benefactors, so be it.

"Okay then," Doc said. "Come on by when you're done here? We haven't seen you in awhile."

"Please do, Gabe," Willow said. "Just wait until you hear about Luna. Doc's about to publish our findings, aren't you Doc?"

"Congratulations," I said.

"And I'm listed as a co-author, aren't I, Doc?"

"Of course you are," he said.

"We're doing an oyster fry this afternoon," Willow said. "Please come. If it wasn't for you, we never would have found Luna."

"I'm pouring bubbly and velvet," Doc said in his deepest, most caressing voice.

"I've got a long day. Three diseased pines to put down. The Orcas Symphony is playing at The Lodge. I promised to be on the dance floor right after the open mic."

"Perfect," Willow said. "We all do the oyster fry and then the open mic. Tollie Stroheim can read her Ode to Luna."

Doc H. made a noise in his deep throat. I read it as derisive of odes to whales. Willow eyed him, her narrow glance. Her shoulders rose. Her tone threatened. "You are coming, too, aren't you, Doc?"

"If you say so, Miss Will." He made a gracious gesture with a swing of his arm but his smile was a rictus that belied the gesture. Doc Hanrahan was not a man who liked to be ordered to do anything.

I trimmed away at dead branches, seething. Aren't you, Doc? Aren't I Doc? Coming, Doc? If you say, so Miss Will. Will: He'd called her Will.

Damned if I'd watch her make a fool of herself at her own oyster fry. Damned if I wouldn't. What difference to me? I debated this all afternoon, felling trees in a fury. It was pathetic, the increasing number of diseased pines I had to put out of their misery. The rage over a situation I was helpless to control was fueled by Miss Will's indifference, or so I now suspect. I laid the pines to rest with my years of professional skill; I could do nothing to defend against a disease that may well wipe out the pine forests of our nation in the decades to come, and most people have no idea it is even here. Were our pines to go the way of the elms?

Doc's party was going good by the time I got there. He loaned me the first cabin next to the Buckhorn Bay Lodge. Doc Hanrahan was fourth generation; his great granddaddy once ran the lodge as a fishing camp. Doc had turned on the old hot water heater and the ancient faucet ran rust for awhile, but a hot shower was a fine tonic to my sore back and aching arms.

From my duffel I dug out my suede jacket, a white shirt with patch pockets that looks half-way dressy, a hand-beaded belt and a pair of turquoise bracelets and found my good snakeskin boots and my dress hand, the one that's useless for work but looks like a suede glove. I never met a tree that complained when I don't shave regular, but I have to admit I looked pretty ratty on four days growth, so I took some time to do a decent shave.

Champagne and black velvet is pretty sissified for Orcas islanders. This is a beer kind of place and there was plenty of that in a cooler by the door but Doc handed me velvet and bubbly and I have to admit that my weakness for the stuff was the main reason I'd come, that and showing them. So what if she was with him? I have no place for a woman in my life. I'm a nomad by instinct and by occupation. When the western forests are too wet to work in winter, I'm having a blast in Hawaii, trimming coffee and macadamia trees, and making side money in surf tournaments.

When the snow blows powdery in Telluride, I'll pop in to visit my dad, where he's got a forty acre, second growth mountainside patch that he bought on the strength of a few good fishing seasons in Alaska. That was twenty years back. Fishing in Alaska hasn't been worth a damn since, or so he likes to tell me, and what do I know? I tried fishing with him one season. Now there is a miserable existence...I'd tossed down a couple of the bubbly and velvets before I'd said two words to anybody at the party.

Willow handed me a plate of tiny, Island-farmed oysters fried in Japanese panko breading; she'd made a slaw that had fat blueberries in it and there was corn on the cob on the side.

A geeky looking guy was setting up a laptop. He'd erected a Power-Point rig in front of what was left of an early day ego wall in Jake Hanrahan's Buckhorn Bay lodge, that would be Doc's grandpa.

Jake was a fishing buddy of my dad's. Between the two of them they taught me how to fish.

The screen obscured the ancient photos and newspaper clippings of sober-faced dudes holding extraordinary salmon catches. Today such catches would get a guy a hefty fine. Today it's all catch and release. The scene in front of me said everything. In the time of our dads and granddads, the sounds and bays were plentiful; today we take pictures and run scientific studies of the scant traces of what's left to catch.

I don't do that much cooking for myself in my camper rig and so I kept sneaking back in the kitchen for more, which is where Willow cornered me and hinted around that she hadn't heard from me in awhile; I said I thought she was tied up with her whale study.

"It's over," she said.

"The Doc?"

She made a face. "Luna," she said. "He's left Waldron. We believe Luna's found his pod."

Doc poked his head into the kitchen. "Will? Gabe? We're ready to roll."

Just before the lights went out, Willow introduced me as the catalyst, how this all began. If not for my offer to show her around Waldron Island, she never would have happened upon Luna the lost whale.

The geeky guy Byron shoved his taped-together glasses up his nose as he stammered through his explanation of what they were about to see, rough footage meant to document the intervention.

"What intervention?" I said to Willow.

"Just watch," she said.

The opening shots were very nice, a beautiful sunrise on a clear day with wisps of fog here and there tucked into the lumps and the rises of the islands, the turtleback curves of hills panning into the curved backs of orca whales as they powered through straits.

"Nice," someone said.

"Not a bad opener," Byron said. "The rest sucks. Don't expect much. I haven't got it together yet."

The film cut to the baby whale, Luna, nudging this vessel and that, hanging around the Waldron dock, waiting to follow any vessel that moved. Much footage of Willow, the pretty girl, leaning over the bow, giving the baby Luna a pat on his head, and of Doc Hanrahan powering the outboard of a Whaler, and additional shots of two research Whalers complete with camera crews shooting footage of each other.

As the footage played, Doc Hanrahan made an opening statement, his body forming a dark blot against the screen. "A baby orca whale living on his own in the wilderness had never been documented in the literature. Orca whales, really over-sized dolphins, are such social creatures that until now, the survival of a killer whale on its own was thought to be impossible.

"Luna, L-98 is a part of the L Pod, one of three orca pods that live in the Pacific Northwest. On August 23," Doc said in his professorial voice, "Luna's pod passed to the west of Waldron Island. This film documents our attempt to lure young Luna close enough to his family's passing pod to perhaps hear and connect with the calls from his family."

At the end of the film, Luna swam away from the Whaler he was following. Doc cut the motor and the Whaler rocked in the tide. The camera passed over a serene, flat calm day, where the water was sleek as some skating rink. Underwater mics caught the eerie sounds of orca calls, lyrical enough that some of our local musicians set them to music, and I heard, to my own satisfaction, at least, the near calls of Luna, and the reply from his pod, and it was a thrilling sight to watch as Willow sat in the bow waving as the baby whale set off toward his pod.

The lights came up. Everyone cheered. Willow poured more of the bubbly and velvet. A chunky young woman dressed in a U-Dub sweatshirt and black jeans with a spiked collar around her neck announced that a blackberry cobbler was being served in the kitchen. There's no finer dessert in creation than blackberry cobbler made from island berries, so plentiful this time of year that they fall off the bushes. It's an odd trick of nature, but our islands are overrun with deer, and the deer won't touch these berries, or believe me, we would not have cobbler.

This woman, Tollie Stroheim, ladled hot cobbler into paper bowls. She had a wonderful ruddy complexion and anthracite eyes set in brick-red cheeks. A single black braid fell down her back. Tollie served the cobbler with dollops of real cream, not that stuff sprayed from a can, all the while muttering dolefully about the film—the human interaction, the petting and stroking of Luna that might lead to rejection by his pod.

Most of us, busy gobbling down the cobbler in the next room, soon heard words between Tollie and Willow, who evidently took Tollie's remarks personally.

"What else could we do?" Willow said. "Leave Luna on his own? Suppose word gets around to some aquarium? You want to see Luna as the star attraction at Water World?"

"The more we treat him like a human infant, the faster he'll become one," Tollie hissed.

Not good. Two women, both right, one stubborn, the other wearing a hobnail collar? I sauntered into the kitchen. "Open mic," I said. "Tollie? They are waiting for you to read your ode." I got hold of Willow and muscled her out of there and marched her to my pickup. She ranted about the audacity of that dyke in the privacy of my truck. Somewhere behind us was a caravan of vehicles. Doc Hanrahan was well back in the pack, escorting Tollie, or so I hoped. We sat in the parking lot until Willow got it all out and then admitted she was ashamed of herself.

When we went inside, Willow gave Tollie a hug and personally announced Tollie's reading from the stage. The young whale, rejected by his pod and turned away by humans, dies of loneliness. The young whale's carcass, toxic from eating contaminated fish, proves to be a waste on fins. Tollie Stroheim's bleak vision evoked gasps and muted applause.

It is a truth of my existence that I am at my most articulate when I am least able to recall exactly what it is I have said, but the stark vision of this stubby woman touched my own. Past counting the bubbly velvets, I got hold of the mic and ranted on about our green island where lightning strikes a stand of dead pines, igniting the deadfall tinder and the island explodes like a fireball turning to ash....

Well, the Orcas Symphony, they know me. We go way back, we go to the time I was the lead dancer in our amateur production of Rent and so they put me through my paces from hornpipes to pow-wows to break dancing, and I set those university smart asses to screaming for me, a man of natural gifts, son of a bareback rider.

Mama taught me to walk fence poles as a toddler before she got tired of motherhood, tired of my dad being gone on his fishing boat most of the year. Mama rejoined the circus, or so Dad said, which is how I took to walking bridge rails, the ridges of roofs, skateboards, surfboards, whatever. I was lonely, looking for my mama, and that night I was full of myself and I loved it when Willow stared at me with a rapturous glow on her face and somehow there were just the two of us, Willow and me left on the floor and all the dances were slow.

"Why did you do it?"

"Do what?"

The lights came up. The room was empty but for the Orcas Symphony putting their instruments away, and nobody paid us any mind, or they pretended not to. Oh, those level brows, they seemed to close over Willow's nose and that intense expression on her face demanded an answer.

"Uncle Charlie said you felled a tree across a power line and lost your hand doing it."

"The power company meant to take all the old growth timber off the road right of ways, and I meant they shouldn't do that."

"So you did mean to do it?"

I mocked her by twirling her under my arm. "I didn't mean to blow off my hand, if that's what you mean."

THE TIME I WAS ROAD KILL

Coach defended me. The ref had been letting the fouls slide. Coach had called it to his attention several times. Coach argued with the principal. What was to be expected from a kid who was being constantly fouled? Still, it did no good. The principal suspended me from the team for the rest of the season. That meant I couldn't play in the biggest home game of the year. Zero tolerance on fighting was the rule.

And that's how I felt. Like a zero. Goose egg. Nada. School and basketball were one and the same and I was old enough to drop out. I t hought it out very carefully. I'd take my GED and bag groceries until I could get into the army or the Peace Corps, whichever would have me.

I told my mom this plan. She was good at listening. I could see the way her mouth turned down at the corners that this decision was hurting her. She asked me to stay in school while she thought what to do. Mom told me not to give up on basketball just yet. She asked me to keep up with practice, even while I was off the team. So I worked on my layups at the basketball hoop above the garage. I went down to the Fun House and dribbled up and down the courtyard. I'd get into scratch games with the older guys.

On Sunday we went out to the Burger Bar for lunch. Mom told me that I could go stay with Uncle Ave. He's not really my uncle, sort of my godfather. We don't seem to have a lot of family. Mom won't talk about it. She said Uncle Ave lives in the mountains of New Mexico. He has these wolves. He sort of got into them by accident. He sprang this wolf out of a trap. She was a female, had a litter of cubs. When the cubs grew up, Ave reintroduced them to the wild. Then the game department found out he had experience with wolves so when they found a wounded wolf, Uncle Ave wound up with it. I could help him with these wolves.

"What would that do? Prepare me for work as a gamekeeper?"

"Maybe," Mom said. "Or a forester. Of course, those people are professionals with college degrees." We bought the full meal with all the trimmings for me. Mom just got one single burger with the meat you can barely see, and some water. No fries. That way the family saves money while I stay thin, Mom likes to say. She used her straw to take a sip of my soda.

"Here's the deal, Jason. If I am going to invest in a plane ticket to New Mexico, you would have to go to school. You would have to play basketball; but here's the catch. You would have to control that temper of yours. Uncle Ave tells me they have just as many blind and dumb refs in New Mexico as they do here." Mom took one of my french fries and sort of teased it over the ketchup the way she does and then she nibbled on it.

"Mom—ohmigod—I'm saved. I'm going to New Mexico and I'm going to play basketball."

"You can play basketball. It's your temper that may lick you."

"I'll control myself. I'll do it. I'll make you proud. I promise."

She smiled, but her eyes were all wet and she rubbed the side of her nose like when her allergies bother her, only it wasn't allergies upsetting her this time. But then I thought about it. We lived ten miles from town. I drove my little sisters home from their cheerleading practice every afternoon. I made their afternoon snacks and saw to it they finished their homework while Mom worked the afternoon and evening shift at the Gas & Stop.

"What will Steffie and Alicia do?"

"We'll find a way. You go on. You make us proud."

As we left the Burger Bar, Sid Loomis, the manager, rushed over to the door, propped it open with his fanny and saluted Mom with his palms together. "Princess Eska," he said in a booming voice that turned heads. Mom laughed. "Thank you, Mr. Loomis."

"My pleasure, Your Highness," he said. "And Jason, boy," he said. "Good luck to a fine young man." I knew for sure by this remark that Sid Loomis had heard that I was ready to drop out of school.

Our car was parked right by the front door and so Mom waved at

Sid as he stood, arms folded, at the front door of the Burger Bar. "Princess Eska of The Northern Water Tribe," I said, imitating Sid's gravelly voice, making Mom laugh as she backed away from the curb.

Sid Loomis is one of our local personalities. He seems to appear at every Island Event. He's never let Mom forget that her unusual name turned up in the animated fantasy cartoon, Avatar: The Legend of Korra; it ran on Nickelodean awhile back. Princess Eska was the talk of Orcas Island High for maybe a day; only Sid Loomis can't seem to let it go. "I think he likes you, Mom."

She rolled her eyes, shook her head. "What's a grown man doing watching some fantasy cartoon on Nickelodean?"

Uncle Ave's log cabin is in the pine forest above this beautiful lake. But New Mexico is a steep state in places and there are these bare highways down below us where there are patches of scab rock and hardly anything else. There's fields around some but the point is, you can see for miles, so I don't know how the animals get caught on the highway and wind up dead. Snakes and squirrels, frogs, skunks, possums and stray dogs, and then the deer. Flattened, mangled and squished. We kept this big trash can tied into the bed of Uncle Ave's pickup and we'd get calls from the highway crew and we'd go out and gather up the dead creatures.

Ave would pull off the highway and send me out with a big square shovel and a broom and he'd tell me to hop to it and I don't mind saying the first few days were bad. First few times I did it, I like to have puked, but I learned to take a deep breath and hold it until the kill was in the back of the truck. I didn't like to go in the pen when the wolves were tearing up the kill, either.

The first few mornings I had to get up at five to go out gathering road kill, I seriously considered turning right around and going back home. First few nights I had nightmares where the headless squirrels, the tail-less snakes and the flattened frogs came after me good and chased me right down the road. Maybe they didn't want to come back and be bothered after they were dead. I don't know, but I was miserable, way sorrier for myself than I ever had been, even when I'd been fresh kicked off the basketball team. We'd toss the contents of the garbage can over the fence to Uncle Ave's wolves and they'd never come near the fence or the road kill until we were gone, but that was okay with me. I didn't want to see anything more because I had to go into the house where my aunt was fixing breakfast and I heard her tell Uncle Ave that she thought there was something seriously wrong with a growing boy who wasn't eating hardly a thing.

I got used to it though, gathering up the road kill. There's no such thing as wolf chow in the supermarket. Uncle Ave wouldn't have approved if there was. He wasn't raising wolves for captivity. He was raising them to go back to the wild.

One day we got a call to head out west of town on Spotted Road and here was this little green bug sitting there, a celery-colored car. You know the type. It looks like a Lego on wheels. I knew whose it was, Kayla Pruitt's. She was the head cheerleader who dated Gavin Mills. He was the center forward on the basketball team. Me, I was way down on the second string. I don't know why, but my shooting was way off and if I got into a game I was lucky to play guard.

The deer was sort of wrapped around the fender of the Lego car, its tongue hanging out. Uncle Ave and I were having an awful time. We had to winch that animal off the car. Kayla must have been going way too fast to have that deer plastered on there like that.

Then, right at the worst possible moment, as Ave and I were throwing the deer into the back of the truck, a big old Dodge Durango pulled up and who should get out the passenger side but Kayla. She had a bandage on her head with her blonde hair falling out.

"Hey, Kayla, I said, "That bandage on you looks like a hat. A beret."

"What would you know about a beret?" It was her boyfriend. I hadn't even seen him get out of the truck.

Kayla was all right but that guy Gavin, he was a wise guy.

"I've got sisters back out on the coast. My older sister has one. She's in college. Her beret has a grosgrain ribbon around the edge. It's sharp."

"Grosgrain is sharp," Gavin mocked.

"Shut up, Gav," Kayla said. "Can't you see Jason is getting that poor dead deer off the car? Look at it, that deer is a young deer. Still with some spots on it, and it jumped out at me. I just froze. I couldn't turn the wheel. Now I've gone and killed the poor thing." Kayla's eyes were all red and her mouth was twisted up ugly and I felt like I wanted to touch her where the bandage was and talk all soothing like I knew to do when one of my little sisters fell off her bike. Kayla turned those big eyes on me then and somehow I saw points of light there in floral patterns, I don't know, like looking into a kaleidoscope.

Then I made the dumbest mistake of the day. I told Kayla about the wolves and how they needed wild meat and invited her and Gavin to come see them sometime.

"Wolves!" Kayla said. "Wolves killed my baby lamb. My dad says the government's stupid, letting wolves run wild again."

"Hey, Kayla, do you know what this guy is doing? He's picking up road kill," Gavin said.

That's how the kids at the school started calling me Road Kill. Damn Gavin started it and the coach happened to be walking by the first time he said it and the other kids slunk off.

Hey Road Kill! Let's shoot some baskets," Gavin taunted. He hated it that Kayla had dissed him over me. Gavin wanted me down. Wanted me finished. I shot real crappy, too, the first few shots. After ten minutes or so, I started to come back. I reached past where the mad sad homesick place was, and felt connected. I was hot. I just dropped those balls from everywhere.

Never could shake the name, but after a while, there was glory added to it. The cheerleaders made up a special call. When I was up on the free throw line they'd lie down and slither on the floor and roll their heads up and then do these back flips going "ROAD KILL." The whole gym would be shouting and I'd sink the shot. Oh they loved me down there and it was a sweet time. I got advanced to the first string. By the end of the season I was a star of the team.

A funny thing. I was doing layups one night behind Lobo's pen and I saw something in his expression. He made this little yip. I went over to the fence and stuck a finger in through the hog wire. Uncle Ave would have killed me for doing such a thing. But Lobo licked my finger. He was just as friendly as a dog.

I don't know what possessed me, but I went around, unlatched the gate, and went in with Lobo. I got down on my knees and he licked my face all over. My aunt Lila came out looking for me to tell me supper was ready.

"Jason Wilson! Just what do you think you are doing? You come out of that cage this minute. That wolf is dangerous. He could jump you any second."

"I can't move, Aunt Lila. Lobo's just eating me up." I was laughing; I could see this big smile on Lobo's face.

Aunt Lila ran and got Uncle Ave. Lobo's hackles came up the minute he saw my uncle. Why Lobo was like that to Uncle Ave and everyone else, I can't say. But that wolf and me, we had a special bond.

One thing I can say about Ave, he understood. He wasn't jealous or upset that I could do with that wolf what he couldn't, but he ordered me to get out of that pen anyway. Over supper he told me that it might be that I could get a scholarship to college to play basketball and I had to think about my future. A wolf is a wild thing. You never know what might set him off. Lobo could attack me and take off my arm, the way it was done to a guy in the next county he'd heard about. Thing was, Ave said, if some wolf took off my arm, just being a wolf, the wolf would be dead and so would my chance to play basketball.

"It isn't just Gabe, you got to look out for, it's your mother and your little sisters," Uncle Ave said. "Your mother Eska, now there's one fine woman. It like to killed her when she lost your daddy."

"Yessir," I croaked.

"Eska Wilson, she just stood up there at your daddy's funeral and said Alan Wilson was a born hero and it was no wonder there in Afghanistan when he sacrificed himself to save his platoon…"

"Yes Sir, Uncle Ave," I said. "You were at the funeral?"

"Of course I was. Oh yes."

"Are you related to the Wilson side of the family?"

"I wish," Ave said. "Your daddy and I went through boot camp together. He was this tall, graceful athletic fellow. I was more of a runt of the litter. Only thing I could beat him at, I was a sharpshooter."

At the end of basketball season, I started to get terrible homesick. It was nice in New Mexico. The mountains are great and I learned to snowboard and ski, but when my sisters called me and told me that a spectacular skateboard park had just been built on Orcas, and there might even be a slot for me on the sailing crew. I just couldn't stand it. I went home for spring semester.

A few months later, I got a call from Uncle Ave. He told me that

Lobo had a girlfriend, a very meek female wolf. She came from some animal park that didn't take good care of its animals. Lobo had a litter and nobody could get near the pups.

"We need you Road Kill," Ave said. It felt funny to hear that name. I'd left the name back in New Mexico, as if it was some special name given me by some New Mexican tribe. I'd shed it like a snake sheds its skin.

"I could come on spring break, Uncle Ave."

"Great. I'll send you a plane ticket."

As soon as I hung up, it hit me. Spring break was when the tournament was coming up at the skateboard park. I was getting better and I thought I might have a shot at getting into the finals. I wanted to call Uncle Ave back and tell him forget it, but how could I do that? Lobo's family needed me.

Mom helped me sort it out. It might work out that Lobo wouldn't know me. If that wolf was just as mean to me as he was to Uncle Ave, why then it would be okay to rewrite my ticket. There was such a thing as trip insurance. I could come home and try out in the skateboard tournament.

"Uncle Ave said he was there at Dad's funeral," I blurted.

Mom said nothing, just sat there, combing her long blonde hair through her fingers like she does when she doesn't know what to say.

"It was Uncle Ave who taught you to salute when the flag was given to me," Mom said.

"I don't know why I don't remember."

"Sometimes our memories are so painful we don't recall them," Mom said, and her eyes fluttered as she turned her face toward the entry hall where a portrait photo of Dad, resplendent in his uniform, hung beside the front door.

"Why did he have to be a hero?" I blurted. "Why didn't he come back home?"

"You know Jason, I have thought about that so many times, but that was the way your dad was made. He was always looking out for somebody else. He'd be the one to help someone change a flat tire or step into the middle of traffic to rescue a confused dog. Once he saw this raggedy guy drop his keys on the sidewalk as he got aboard a city bus. This was down in Burlington. I was carrying you and we were late to the doctor's. Here's this fellow, had a big garbage bag with him. Full of bottles he'd collected, if I had to guess. Your dad chased that bus through terrible traffic before we caught up with it, and I gave him a hard time because we were late to the doctor's office and got rescheduled. And then there was the time this RV pulled off the road. Dad saw flames on the undercarriage. He managed to get the family out of the car before the engine exploded."

New Mexico in the spring, the air is so bright with snow melting off in patches. There are all these delicate flowers, alpine flowers, different from the ones here on the island, where we have way more cultivated gardens full of iris and roses and such.

It's a sixty mile drive from Uncle Ave and Aunt Lila's to the airport. They both came to get me. We talked some the first few minutes, but there was this tension, this silence. It was as if we were all thinking the same thing. What about Lobo? Would he remember me? Or would he try to take my arm off?

I didn't even try to get my luggage out of Ave's truck. As we approached the cage, Lobo's ears went down flat. His lips curled back and those teeth, they weren't friendly.

But then Uncle Ave had an idea. "We're going to back off, son, but we'll be right here if you need us." So I went up to the cage alone. I put up the back of my hand and Lobo sniffed at it, and then he licked my fingers through the wire and before Uncle Ave could do a thing about it, I was inside the cage and had my arms around that wolf. I got down on my knees and gave him a big hug, and Uncle Ave and Aunt Lila were cheering, quiet little cheers. "Way to go, Road Kill!"

The pups were just the cutest things. The mama went right off, back into her corner and I could play with the pups as much as I wanted. I'd get my sleeping bag and spend the night with Lobo and his family and I'd wake up with a pup asleep on my face.

That was a sweet time, they were sweet animals. Where they are, I don't know and I'm not sure Uncle Ave does either.

When the cubs were big enough Uncle Ave opened the cage and those wolves were gone, faded right into the woods behind Uncle Ave's barn. But when I think back on the time I was Road Kill, I like it just fine.

SAVING THE ANGEL

The knock came at our door around seven a.m., a gentle tapping. Beside me, Ben moaned and tried to roll over, but his injured knee was trapped in a wedge of pillows.

"Don't you move. I'll get it." I wrapped myself in my red fleece robe, ran a hand through my rumpled hair, and went to the front door.

"Mornin' ma'am," said an angular fellow in an amiable tone. He doffed an enormous, battered Stetson that seemed too important, or perhaps simply too large, for his head. "Is Mr. Bridges home?"

"He's not up yet," I said, peering into this stranger's narrow face. Bareheaded, he was a craggy composition of bony brow and hollow cheek. He had a domineering, beaky nose and a defiant knot of a chin. Since I wasn't wearing my contact lenses, he seemed fuzzy of face, but even so, I was aware of a glint in his limpid black eyes.

"Dang it, I'm sorry. I know Mr. Bridges is usually up and working by this time. I'm Eddie Zellwin, by the way. I worked for Mr. Bridges last summer. Always did know Mr. Bridges had some project or other going. Never did see nobody outwork that man and, well, I just got back from Europe. Somebody nabbed my wallet in Holland. Tell him it's his ole' buddy Eddie, but everbody calls me Bones. Tell him Bones come on by. I helped him lay this flagstone walk you got here?"

"Let me see what Ben says." I smiled to myself. Our flagstone walk, with its meticulously laid stones, was a project Ben had done last spring while I was away. I had often wondered how Ben had done the work by himself. I left Bones at the door, hired as far as I was concerned. Fifty people were arriving come sundown and Ben, our head chef, was out of commission.

A grimace stained Ben's face as he struggled to sit up. The white rings around his eyes and the gritting of teeth when he thought I wasn't looking betrayed his agony. "Who is it?"

"Bones. He says he helped you lay the flagstone walk?" I was careful to keep a neutral tone. When Ben is down it's never smart to take control of the ship.

"Ask him to come back at ten."

Rearranging my robe to look less disheveled, I returned to the front door and relayed Ben's message. "No problem, ma'am. Thank you kindly. I'll surely be here." Bones swept his Stetson from his head. I was smitten. The man had manners. I watched him leave. He was quick about it, a good sign. This was not a lazy person; a drifter he might be, but not feckless.

I returned to the bedroom bearing an ice pack from the freezer. "Bones must be starving. So emaciated."

"He's just a skinny guy." Ben winced as I raised the covers and installed the cold pack on his swollen knee. I'd called Doc Crocker last night. Ben was not to think of getting out of bed. Orcas Island, here in the American San Juans, boasts an old-fashioned doctor you can call at home. Doc Crock, as he is known, was also coming to the party.

"Maybe there's something Bones could do," I hinted, in lieu of what I thought. We were saved. A scrawny angel had been sent to our door. Bones was divine intervention. To say such a fool thing would queer the deal with Ben, however, so I kept mum.

"Get in here," Ben muttered through chattering teeth. "Come warm me."

The woeful Ben of seven a.m. was not the wounded knight who greeted Bones at ten. Ben was combed, shaved, dressed in his denims, and finished with his breakfast. He sipped black coffee pressed from fresh beans. Though he argued about it, I insisted he keep a pillow under his knee. His lame leg was stretched over a second chair at the dining table.

At the stroke of ten by the antique clock on the wall, Eddie Zellwin appeared, our angel, also known as Bones. Ben smoked one of his wretched cigars. Bones rolled a cigarette and brought Ben up to speed. His backpack was snatched while he was on the phone in Holland. We saw snapshots of his European tour and a photo of Bones with his daughter, a thin toddler with a bright smile that seemed wider than her face.

"She has your bright eyes," I said to Bones.

"That's my daughter Mandy and this here's my ex," Bones said, his long face doleful. "She didn't want to be married no more. Wanted back to the swingin' life." Bones' ex-wife, wide, blonde and sturdy, was posed on a sidewalk in jeans and a sweater, forcing a smile at the camera. Or maybe it was just that the sun was in her eyes. But at any rate, she looked too sensible to want to run back to the single life, toddler in hand.

Ben went on and on, asking about Bones' family, people I knew nothing about and never heard mentioned before. Finally, and none too soon, to my way of thinking, Ben turned the conversation around to our predicament. "Fifty people will be arriving around—what time did you tell them?"

"Any time after sunset," I said.

"Sundown and this place is a madhouse," Ben said, orchestrating a chaotic scene with his cigar as a baton. "My trick knee gave out yesterday. We were on the mainland loading supplies. I stumbled off the sidewalk. Made a complete fool of myself. Can't stand up on the thing. I'm supposed to be making a pot of gumbo. I've got most of the shrimp but nary a crab."

"Don't you worry Mr. Bridges," Bones said. "I can do that. I might have been raised in Galveston, but mama's people come from the bayou. I make gumbo the right way, like our grandma did."

"The okra," Ben said.

"And the crab, the shrimp, and the roux. I know it all."

"And you sauté the onions first?" Ben said.

"Onions? No sir," Bones' eyes widened. "Can't use regular onions. In Louisiana that's dang near 'gainst the law. The onions got to be green onions. Scallions. That's how we do it. Chopped in bitty little pieces and sautéed till you smell their perfume. Then you dust them with the gumbo filet powder."

Ben puffed on his cigar and thought awhile. "I believe you are right, Bones. You are hired." From Ben's grand tone, you would have thought Bones had just been made head chef at a five star restaurant in the French Quarter.

Ben might have injured his knee, but his gift for people was intact. A gift that in some ways I personally believed was a curse. Ben had hired hundreds of workers in his time, and he had a way of making each one feel special, as if he were working for an uncle, or a daddy. It wasn't just Ben that Bones was working for. Bones was working for his honor and that of his daughter, and his sister and brother-in-law who had a business in Redmond and his daddy with his barge business in Galveston and on and on. Before that slow and seemingly casual conversation had ended, Bones had been massaged by the master. He was going to produce the best danged gumbo the San Juan Islands had ever seen.

The downside to all this was, of course, that Ben's paternalism was no act. He had a genuine interest in all sorts coupled with an egalitarian philosophy. It didn't matter to Ben if a guy was penniless or had just gotten out of jail. Any person who pledged to better himself was okay by Ben. It never seemed to occur to him that promises could be broken, however. Consequently, he had been ripped off, stolen from, and lied to more times than I could count and I'd be left with Ben's howls of anguish and rage. By the time Bones came along I was convinced that among the needy and the downtrodden there was an underground railroad with the Orcas Island stop being Ben. On the other hand, due to our desperate circumstances and his fortuitous timing, I set Bones apart in my mind as a special dispensation. Bones was a gift, a lucky break, an angel indeed.

"Not enough crab?" Bones added. "Leave that to me. I'll bring you crab not ten minutes out of the sound."

Ben eased the gray ash off the end of his cigar, laying a length of it whole in the ashtray as if it were a complete thought. As if nothing less was expected. As if the appearance of this Samaritan was totally in keeping with the cycle of our destiny.

"I'll show up for the party dressed proper in dark slacks with a white shirt and tie. I plan to locate here on Orcas, and I want to get me a good job with the Willard Hotel. I brung along my resort clothes," Bones said.

His tux? His blazer? His boater and white linen pants? I wondered. "And where are you staying?"

"Why ma'am, I been camping out over at the Moran State Park. It's just wonderful out there. The smell of them cedars? There's nothing like that back in Texas."

By noon Bones came in with a writhing gunnysack full of crabs. I dug out our enormous speckled enamel pot, battered from years of use. Bones boiled the crabs while Ben supervised, and the three of us picked crabs until our fingers were sore. Bones cut his thumb and I poured peroxide on it and bandaged it. Bones kept right on working, despite the nasty cut.

Our son Jeff, home from college and working at the Willard for the summer, brought in the padded chairs we kept out in the garage for serious events. Ben had acquired the chairs from the Willard when it was bought out and redecorated for the fifth time. Or the sixth, I forget which.

My friend Ellie Hawke came early in the afternoon. She's a caterer; she does the most lavish weddings on the island. Ellie supervised the layout of the bar, but Bones had taken over the kitchen and so she stepped aside while Bones got the roux going. Around four o'clock, there was a dicey moment when Bones declared the roux a disaster. "This just ain't right," he said. "It's been awhile since I done this, and the roux ought to have a better color."

"Where did you find him?" Ellie hissed. "Do you think he's just out of jail?"

"He's all right," I said. "Ben is a very good judge of these things."

Ellie flounced her sleek black curls and rolled her eyes at me when Bones flushed the whole roux down the sink. We fished another pound of butter out of the freezer and Bones started over.

"I didn't cook the fat quite enough. It's got to be a pecan brown," he assured Ben. "I'm sorry Mr. Bridges, but I do believe you'd want me to do it the right way."

"Go right ahead, Bones." Ben lit another cigar and shifted on his pillows. With Ellie Hawke kneading his neck, he was having a grand time.

Within the hour, Bones delivered a bowl of the roux to Ben for a tasting. He said it was fine and to proceed with the rest of it. Since the roux redux had run us into sunset, guests arrived just as Bones was adding the filet powder to the mix. The entire house took on the rich ambiance of some Basin Street bistro. Son Jeff had found just the right jazz for the occasion and guests arrived bearing fancy appetizers, salads and breads, which we squeezed onto the table, adding to a mountain of food Ellie and I had prepared.

Ben deigned to take a pain pill so that he could hobble around on crutches. I told and retold the story of how this unlikely angel, Bones, had arrived in a providential manner to save the occasion for us. Bones' gumbo was a smash hit. I was horrified to see that he'd plunked the battered porcelain pot on the buffet table, ignoring the pottery casserole, handmade here on the island, which I had set out. I didn't see what he'd done until it was too late; but nobody seemed to care, and as the stock got low, guests would sidle over to the pot and tip it to spoon out the dregs.

As hard as he worked at the party, Bones got out and hustled. Ben had lent him our half-finished guesthouse to sleep in and a sleeping bag. Next morning, Bones was up for coffee when we were. He was extremely fond of our Jamaican blue mountain coffee, squeezed in a French press. In Bones' Texas drawl, this became "blue mauca," and so Bones stayed on and never returned to his campsite at Moran State Park.

It took Bones a few days of continuous calling to land himself an interview at the Willard Resort. Bones had acquired his persistence as a salesman at his brother-in-law's used car lot down in Redmond, Microsoft country, you know. Bones was named best salesman a couple of years back, which satisfied my curiosity. I wondered how he had been able to spend the last six months touring Europe.

The ingratiating Bones talked his way onto the Willard bell staff, and threw himself into the work. He spoke of the "Willard concept of service" and the "Willard ideal." I was impressed to hear all of this. For most of its life, the Willard white elephant of a mansion had struggled as a hotel. The Willard family had long since sold off the hundreds of acres surrounding the hotel to recreational housing developments. The hotel tottered along under one management after another. After the Bank of America foreclosed on it, some Arabs had it for awhile; then a Japanese investment group paid an exorbitant price for it. Finally, they unloaded it on this new outfit, the Willard Resorts, which, as it turned out, had actual money with which to renovate the place and a professional marketing division that focused on uppity yuppies and the hyper rich.

Bones seemed to know just how to handle his job. "These are wealthy people who are spending a bundle and what I do is help them feel special and rich," he told us, soon after he started his job. Hefty tips lined Bones' pockets. He landed a coveted assignment as factotum to a Microsoft convention and when a glowing report about Bones landed on the manager's desk, he came within an inch of being elevated into management.

"They want to give me a title and work me eighty hours a week at minimum wage. There's just no way I can do it," he moaned to Ben one morning when his shift had been moved from the six a.m. to the four p.m. The hotel had him working the craziest hours, sometimes until after midnight, ending a twelve-hour day, whereupon he was to be up at six thirty to meet some party of muck-a-mucks arriving on the ferry. I tried to warn Bones that only a robot could keep such hours, but he brushed me off. "I need me a place before winter. When low season comes, Willard Resorts transfers their best people to their place down in the Florida Keys. I aim to be one of them. I'm in heaven, ma'am. Boy howdy."

Bones soon discovered the classic island problem: there's nothing available for workers to rent in high season. Bones qualified to live in the dorms that the Willard resort provided, but this meant camping in with scores of young kids who raised hell all night. Bones, in his thirties, needed his sleep. Living in our primitive quarters was not what he had in mind, either. Within three weeks, he came up with an ingenious solution. He bought a boat, a fifty-foot fishing trawler, which he purchased for a mere five thousand dollars. He came to the house for some of the blue mauca. "With the kind of money I'm making," he bragged to Ben, "I'll have her free and clear come November. Then I'll get some of the boys from the hotel and we'll run her down to Baja."

Ben reveled in Bones' success. He'd gone down with Bones to inspect the craft. The seller had bought the vessel from a fisherman with the intent of restoring her, only to find out what an enormous job it was. Ben, who certainly should have known better, was thrilled. Ben cannot live without a boat; we'd sold our Hatteras last summer and Ben had bought an Albin 28 to putter around in as soon as my back was turned. The men had gone through two pots of mauca while they talked of batteries, fuel pumps, fenders, power supplies, mooring line, and bilge pumps.

"Tell me. What does Bones know about boats?" I said after he left. I might as well have fallen off the dock and gone down for the third time. Ben's face radiated the idiot's gleam that comes over boaters—an addled breed.

"Bones made a hell of a buy," he said.

"The fuel," I sighed. "It'll take him a week's pay just to fill the tanks."

"Bones isn't going anywhere. He lives aboard, Carla. He's already got a buddy lined up to move in, an English guy. He'll have help with the payments. A fifty-footer for rent money? I call that a hell of a deal."

To save on moorage fees, Bones put the big gray hulk on a mooring buoy out in the bay—just whose buoy it was, nobody knew. Ben loaned him a propane stove. But when Bones next reported how he had bought a 12-volt TV set, Ben, unaccountably, turned peevish. I should have seen the warning flags right then.

"A 12-volt TV set costs hundreds of dollars. That's how these kids are. They have to make payments on the vessel, but they run out and buy a TV set," Ben groused. We happened to be out on the Albin, setting out crab traps near Pole Pass when the subject came up.

"They can't afford to fill the fuel tank and go anywhere," I said. "They might as well watch TV like every other live-aboard I ever knew." Including us, I could have added, recalling our dock-bound days. I was on deck, righting the big wire trap, getting ready to toss it off the stern. I was shouting to make myself heard over the clatter of the diesel engine, which wasn't running well. Ben was at the helm, down in the cabin.

"Bones doesn't even have a dinghy and he buys a TV set," Ben shouted back.

So how does he get to work?" I said in what I hoped passed for a reasonable tone. Ben stared at me, letting me read his mind.

"You loaned Bones our dingy?" I screeched.

He raised his hands from the wheel, capitulating, lest I throw the crab trap at him. I might have done it, too. Problem was, I couldn't stuff a truck-tire-sized trap through the cabin hatch. The cowering Ben, comically bugging his eyes, was safe from my wrath.

"It's not as if we are using the dinghy right now," Ben shouted over the diesel roar.

"That's not the point and you damn well know it, Ben," I yelled back. This was shorthand for what I didn't have to remind him. The last time he lent out our dinghy, it had been returned sans the cowling off the top of the outboard. The new cowling cost us two hundred dollars.

Bones came around Friday morning to grind up some odd-looking roots. Thistle weed he said. It was great for your health. His, maybe, I decided, when I saw the stuff. He pulverized it in my food mill. Then he stowed the thistle weed in the trunk of our old Triumph and drove off. We keep an extra car around for when we have houseguests. That way they can drive themselves to the top of Mt. Constitution to admire the view. The Triumph is usually parked in the boater's lot down at the harbor, which is why I had not realized that Bones had not only our dinghy for transportation but also the use of our Triumph.

"Bones had to sell his car to come up with the down payment on the boat," Ben said. "You've never had to struggle for anything, Carla. You don't understand what guys have to go through."

"But I do understand what we have to go through," I snarled. "Remember the Caddy, Ben? Have you forgotten the Beemer?" He'd once loaned an old Cadillac to a boy who worked in our warehouse. Boy and Caddy promptly disappeared. The car had turned up in a drug raid in Denver. Ben had been reluctant to file a stolen vehicle report; therefore Ben had been implicated in the drug raid and we'd had to pay our attorney three times what the car was worth to sort the matter out.

And the little Beemer? That had gone to a young couple Ben knew slightly. He worked in construction and she was a hardware clerk. I begged Ben not to co-sign a loan for the car. They made a few payments, then moved to Butte and our very own bank made us pay back the loan on our own car. The title remained with the kids who'd ripped us off. We dropped about thirty five hundred that time.

"We don't know Bones that well. Suppose he wrecks the car?" I said. Ben just waved me away as he came topside to drop the crab trap over the side.

Later that week, Bones sipped mauca, rolled a smoke, and told us how Cap'n Jan had come aboard and gotten his diesel to purring. She installed two extra bilge pumps.

"I heard there was a new mechanic in Deer Harbor," Ben said.

"Yes sir, and she's a dandy. Six three if she's an inch with a pair of hands she could use for serving platters."

"I wouldn't want to argue with her," Ben said.

"No, sir. I believe Cap'n Jan holds her own on the dock."

Bones' next problem was, his decrepit trawler was in dire need of a haulout. "The way the water seeps in the bottom, I think them cracks must be wider than the planks," Bones moaned. Ben gave him a pep talk about how he could take the big boat out to one of the uninhabited islands and beach her while he caulked the bottom with the help of a few kids from the resort; a keg of beer and a promise of the Baja trip. That would do the trick.

A few days later, Bones showed up with his new shipmate. Alex, his name was. Alex wanted work. Anything Ben thought he was worth was all right with him. Alex's Yorkshire accent was so thick I frequently had to translate for Ben. Alex was missing two front teeth. He was never without a thick wool cap that leaked a few scraggly curls, from which I inferred he was bald. He had a knot of a scar over his cheekbone. Though scrawny of build and dressed like a vagrant, Alex allowed how he loved the glamour sports. He was into skiing, and he raced cars and motorcycles. His movements were slow and stiff because at one time or another, he'd broken every bone in his body. Hearing this news, I squinted at Ben. He knew what I meant: Thank God we had no race cars or motorcycles to lend out.

Alex put in a week's work and was to be at the house early on Monday. We were going off-island after a load of shrubs from a mainland nursery and had to make the red-eye. Alex was to drive our old truck while Ben drove the Jeep. Monday came but Alex didn't. Ben drove the truck; I drove the Jeep. We barely made the eight p.m. return ferry and weren't back on the island until nine thirty. There was an ominous message on our answering machine. The Willard Resort was looking for Bones.

Alex finally showed up midday Tuesday. He said that Bones and he had gone to Friday Harbor Sunday and missed the last ferry back. Bones was down with something, quite possibly the flu.

"Not the Irish flu?" I said.

"No, no, nothing like that," Alex assured me. "Bones is not much on the drink."

Meanwhile our son Jeff had been transferred into the fine dining section of the Willard—as a mere busboy, to his chagrin. "The waiters they hire?" he told me, "They do this training session where they taste all the wines."

"I do hope they know you are only eighteen," I said.

"Yeah, Mom, but the bartender likes me. She said she'd slip me a whole bottle—just kidding, Mom." He trumped my horrified reaction by opening the refrigerator door and swigging orange juice right out of the bottle, daring me to bitch about that.

"And how is Bones doing? Have you seen anything of him?"

"He hasn't been there for a few days. Somebody said they fired him."

"What a shame. He was such a devoted employee."

Bones came by the house a few days later, spiffy in his white shirt and tie. The Willard's section manager had driven clear over here to Deer Harbor to talk him into coming back to work.

"I called in sick. I told them I'd been to the doctor. Maybe they didn't get the message. Maybe they didn't believe me," Bones said, sipping his mauca. "But the manager had a stack of referral cards from the guests. I'm being put up for employee of the month."

"Those strange hours, Bones," I said. "Can't they give you a regular schedule?"

"Why, ma'am, I'd do anything for the Willard. Thursday night they are putting me up so that I can serve as personal escort to Mrs. Randolph Willard. She's coming in on her private yacht. I think I'll call my dad. He'd be as proud as can be." This announcement was doubly startling. Mrs. Randolph Willard? The Willards?

Here also was something new about Bones and his father. Bones had said his father was a wealthy Texan who owned an enormous barge business in Galveston. He had also claimed his old man used to beat his mother and had abandoned her and left her destitute. But now Bones was calling his dad. He wanted approval from this man? As Bones left, I happened to see him hand Ben some money. And Ben happened to see me watching him.

"All right!" he sputtered as soon as the door closed on Bones' back. "I loaned Bones some money to put down on his boat."

I simply clutched my mouth and sighed. After I had banged around in the kitchen for a while, I stomped into Ben's den. "How much this time?"

"Just a thousand dollars—Bones is a good boy. He works hard. He's already paid me back a couple of hundred."

"Bones lost his wallet three days ago. I loaned him a hundred and fifty."

Bones assured me he would have the money back to me come

payday Friday, but we didn't see him that day, nor did Alex. So I asked Alex how Bones was. "He hasn't been doing so well lately. So he's been staying with a lady friend of his in town."

"Well that's good. It saves the long drive up to the resort."

At lunch, Alex announced that they wouldn't need our dinghy any longer. "Bones got himself the most beautiful Zodiac. His buddy, an ex-airline pilot, made him a special deal. Five hundred and it's worth twenty seven hundred if a ha'penny."

Ben and I stared at each other. If Bones now had a fancy Zodiac to pay for, it was unlikely that we would be receiving payments on our investment anytime soon. A couple of days later, I inquired after Bones' health while Alex was helping me mulch the yard.

"He's not at all well," Alex said. "He did come back to the boat, but he's too weak to get up." That afternoon I made some chicken soup and sent it home with Alex.

"Make sure Bones takes his fluids, would you?"

"Oh, you do look after Bones, now don't you, Carla?"

On Friday, Ben took Alex down to Deer Harbor. The two of them were going to assist Cap'n Jan with our Albin, which was behaving sluggishly; but Ben called me not ten minutes later. "Call Doc Crock. Tell him I'm bringing Bones in. We found him hunched over on a bench on the dock, looking like death. Hasn't kept food down in three days."

"So he's dehydrated, then?"

"I don't know, Carla. Maybe it's food poisoning."

It was eight p.m. by the time they got back. Jeff was away for the weekend, so we put Bones into Jeff's bedroom downstairs. I invited Alex to supper, but he wouldn't hear of it. He took off on foot for the harbor. I'd thawed out more of the chicken soup and Ben and I had some of it.

"What did you find out?"

"It's hepatitis C."

"That's terrible. Are you sure? Is that what Doc said?" Ben glared at me. He detests my terrible need to confirm everything.

"Doc wouldn't tell me a thing."

"Confidentiality, Ben. We aren't relatives."

"Bones admitted it once Alex and I got him back in the car. Turns out he's had hepatitis C for years. He's on disability and Medicaid."

"Hepatitis C? Isn't that the nasty one?"

"Bones is a very sick boy."

Then I remembered that Doc Crocker himself had been at the party. Doc knew Bones' condition. He would never have put fifty people at risk.

Jeff came home after eleven. He'd gone on a boat cruise to Victoria with his buddies at work and gone straight to the resort. We hadn't seen him in three days. I told him Bones would be in his bed for the night and he'd have to sleep in Ben's den.

"Hey, Mom, no problem." He was sprawled on the couch, leafing through the latest issue of *Wired*. I couldn't tell whether he was paying attention, but I told him about the hepatitis C. And how it was spread.

"And how are things at the Willard?"

"Oh, guess what, Mom. The owner was there, this little old lady. Mrs. Willard. Somebody said she was married to a famous politician." Alexander Hay Willard. Scion of one of the wealthiest and most blue-blooded of American families. Ambassador to Britain. A Senate majority leader, back in the seventies. A cold war hawk who was hot for the ladies. Rumored to have died in the bed of a network TV reporter, but my son didn't have to know that. "Mrs. Hay had dinner in the dining room," Jeff said. "She wore this cool gray suit. Had this diamond ring on that was as big as my fist. I was her busboy. She smiled at me when I cleared the plates. Pretty chintzy though. She didn't leave a big tip."

"I wouldn't think the owner would have to tip in her own dining room….Poor Bones. He was supposed to have been her personal escort, and here he is, barely able to sit up. He wanted so badly to do well at the Willard." I wondered whether Bones had called his father? I hoped not.

"Yeah, Mom, I know you like Bones and so do I. But Bones blew his second chance. He was assigned to look after some of those rich kids while their parents were out on a fishing trip. The resort put him up so he'd be sure and make the outing. He was supposed to be ready at six. By ten a.m. they had to call his room and wake him up."

"He's a sick person. He needs stable hours."

"But Bones brought some of it on himself. The night he spent at the resort? He was drinking wine with the late crew and they all stayed up until after two."

On Bones' second morning in the house, I sent Jeff downstairs to try to reason with him. He had to eat. An hour or so later, shaved and dressed, Bones came jauntily up the stairs with assistance from Jeff.

"You're looking much better, Bones."

"Thank you, Mrs. Bridges."

"Will you have some oatmeal?"

"I believe I will. And do you have any of that blue mauca?" Jeff had a date to go kayaking. Ben and I lingered at the table with Bones

"What are you going to do now?" Ben said

."I don't rightly know," Bones said. "I've got one hefty paycheck coming from the Willard while I decide."

"This is a blessing in disguise, Bones. You can't collect disability payments while working. The government might prosecute and then where would you be?"

"Doc Crock tells me I shouldn't work. But what they pay on disability, a dog couldn't live on."

"Do odd jobs. Off the books," Ben said.

"Try the tour guides at the harbor. You are such a good talker, one of them is sure to take you," I said.

"There are dozens of boats down there and every one of them needs some kind of maintenance. Talk to Cap'n Jan. She'll find work for you. Something you can do at your own pace," Ben said.

"I hate the boat. I have to get off it!" Bones' face was a mask of pain.

"Are you having problems with it?" Ben said.

"The problem is me. It's too cold on there. The water's always coming in, never stops. I have nightmares that I'm drowning."

"The seller warned you she's got to be caulked. He didn't lie." I said.

Ben glowered at me. I always had to be summing up the obvious.

"How much do you owe on it?" Ben said.

"Fifteen hundred."

"You could sell that Zodiac, pay off everybody and come up with enough to buy a beater car."

"And let down my pilot friend? He told me he'd sell that Zodiac to me and me alone at that price." Bones got out a ratty pouch, dribbled tobacco into a rolling paper trough and without wasting a crumb, rolled a cigarette, licking the paper to seal the smoke. He fired up his cigarette, lighting it with a match from a gold-embossed book from the Willard Hotel.

"God bless that Zodiac. That's a mighty vessel," he said, gazing into space. "Me and Alex were sitting out on the deck of the trawler one evening last week when we heard these cries off in the distance. First I thought it was gulls after a run of smelt. You know how they can screech when they get to fighting over lunch. Then I realized it was voices: cries for help, clear down by Pole Pass. So me and Alex jumped in that Zodiac and took off like we was shot. Found a boat overturned and two boys fighting to make it to shore but the current was against them and they was done in. Alex and me, we dragged them kids aboard the Zodiac and rounded up their dinghy for them, and all I can say is, we were glad to be there to help."

"You may well have saved those two boys, Bones," I said. "But now you have to save yourself. As for letting down your pilot friend, does he have a clue how sick you are?"

"Nobody knows. Ya'll are the only ones on the island."

"Don't you have family in Redmond?"

"My brother-in-law and sister. I can't intrude on them," Bones said.

"This is illness, not imposition," I said. "Bones, you have to have the best medical help. The University in Seattle has one of the great hospitals in the country."

"They have a hepatitis clinic. Doc wants me to do a tissue biopsy. He thinks my liver's half done for, stiff as old shoe leather. He wants me on the transplant list."

I marched into Ben's study, grabbed the remote phone and handed it to Bones. "Let's do that right now and get it out of the way. These things are tricky. A donor liver has to match up with your blood type. Have you read the CDC reports on the internet?" I didn't tell Bones what else it said. Half the time a matched liver wouldn't take. Even if a match was found, Bone's chance of survival was a grim fifty percent.

Alex arrived, ready for work. Ben invited him in for coffee. "I left the heat going on the boat. You'll be comfy," he said to Bones.

"I don't believe I could make the boarding ladder," Bones said. "My legs ain't quite as stable as two rubber bands. I believe I'll call Billie. She keeps a bed for me at her place—my own bed," he said, sheepishly. "A hell of a thing. My age and I can't even get close with anybody." He wiped a tear off his cheek and immediately pulled himself together. "A beautiful day here, ain't it?"

"Keep after him Alex," I said later, as he helped me plant clumps of petunias. "He has got to get on that transplant list."

"I'll mention it, Carla," Alex growled. "But I'm Bones' friend, not his nanny."

Alex didn't come to work Monday but we were used to that. We figured he drank too much over the weekend. Anywhere else, we'd have canned Alex long since. In the San Juan Islands in high season, however, it is impossible to find anyone to do anything. Ben was hobbling around on his bad knee and couldn't keep up with the yard work. That's why he insisted that we feed Alex a good lunch and cut him miles of slack.

On Tuesday, Ben noticed that our Triumph was not parked at the marina. When he inquired on the dock, the hands had seen neither Bones nor Alex in several days. When Bones failed to show up Friday morning to grind his thistle weed, I called the sheriff's department here on Orcas and the jail in Friday Harbor. Neither Bones nor Alex had been picked up. I informed the sheriff's office that we were going to board the trawler because the bilges would have to be pumped out.

Deer Harbor was glass, the tide way out, and Bones' trawler bobbed at anchor. As our outboard churned through the thickened water, I remembered what Bones had told us, his story of rescuing the two boys with the overturned boat. Suppose Bones and Alex took to speeding in that Zodiac and flipped it in the channel? Had the rescuers gone the way of the rescued? I shook off this ominous inner vision. But then, as we approached Bones' gray hulk, I saw with great relief that the Zodiac was not missing at all. It had been hauled up on the rear deck of the trawler. This meant that someone in the harbor must have given them a ride to the dock. Since the Triumph was gone, Bones and Alex must have taken it off island.

Ben went below to check the bilges while I climbed into the wheelhouse. It was about what you might expect, a rummage of dirty laundry, unwashed plates, a half-eaten pizza, empty beer cans and the sort of gear that clutters boats: batteries, oil, flashlights, boots, and slickers. There were overdue videos from the rental store, including "How to have Great Sex." In a kitchen drawer I found what I was looking for, a list of phone numbers. I copied them down on a paper napkin.

"It's a good thing we came when we did," Ben said. "The bilges weren't a spit from overflowing."

We went to sleep that night on a plan. I'd call the numbers I'd scribbled on the napkin. If we turned up no one who had heard from Bones, we'd file a report that the Triumph was missing. Not that we thought Bones would steal it, but suppose he and Alex had run off the road? People could vanish off the Interstate.

A dazzle of a moon arose overhead. By the green eyes of the bedside clock it was midnight. I hadn't slept at all. Ben was snoring softly and I got up to close the blinds. Bones' predicament came back to me, how little we knew of him, and how inept, how inappropriate, had been our help. Ben had a soft spot for needy, stray people. I suppose he was paying back for all the people who had helped him when he founded the first of a string of successful businesses. But so often his attempts to help proved wrong. What had he done but put Bones into a situation that was impossible for him to cope with?

I crawled into bed and confessed to the clock. I'd allowed my husband to pull another Roxie situation. Roxie had been Ben's shop assistant back when we ran Consolidated Electric down in Renton. She'd been forthright about her drinking problem and so Ben had hired her and she was a wonderful worker. But Roxie's sister was rearing her children and she wanted them back. Roxie kept after Ben until he put up money for a bigger apartment, bought three plane tickets and had our lawyer arrange for a transfer of custody. The children glared at Ben as they got off the plane. Roxie got drunk in the ladies' room and in less than a month the children were back with their aunt. What had our meddling done for Roxie but confirm her inadequacies?

What had we done for Bones but buy him a lifestyle he couldn't cope with?

I was still in my red fleece robe next morning when the ship's bell clanked out on the porch, our island version of a doorbell. Ben answered the door: "Well my gosh. Here you are. Were we ever worried about you!"

"Yes sir, Mr. Bridges, I know I done the wrong thing. Alex kept after me to call, so you can't blame him. It was all my fault." Bones was dressed in starched whites and managed to convey his usual upbeat attitude.

"We thought you'd flipped the Zodiac out in the channel," I said. Despite my waspish tone, I found myself pouring blue mauca for Bones and getting out the cream he loved.

"Well, sir, I have to admit, I went down to Redmond to see my sister. I thought she and my brother-in-law might loan me the money to get out from under the boat."

"Would it have been too much to call?"

"That's enough, Carla," Ben hissed. "Bones knows he should have called us." We all sat silently around the table. Finally, Ben said: "Now, Bones, what is it that you need?"

"I still owe fifteen hundred on the boat, a thousand to ya'll, and I have got to get me some sort of car. I sat up talking to my sister all one night, and I about had her convinced she'd help me out, but damned if she didn't change her mind." He stirred his mauka, gathering his thoughts. "My sister said she ain't going to bail me out of no mess I got myself into off in the San Juan Islands. She wants me to move in with her and her family."

"Your sister is right. She's a woman with good sense," I said. "You are a sick person and she wants to give you the care you need."

Bones brow crimped. His mouth drew down. "I can't live off my sister."

"What does she do? Does she have a family?"

"Yes ma'am. She's studying something about computers. She has two children in middle school."

"So? You could be of great help to her on the days you feel good."

"You know how to sell cars." Ben added.

"I'm going to talk to Cap'n Jan," Bones said. "She knows my boat inside out. She might know somebody willing to take it on. Then I think I'll head down to Colorada. I want to see my daughter. I just know Mandy misses me."

Within the week, Cap'n Jan took over the trawler. She traded Bones her decrepit car for the down payment and gave the trawler owner a promissory note. She announced she had plans for the vessel. Ben was very relieved. At least the old trawler went into capable hands. It was a Friday. Bones came to talk to us and grind his thistle weed.

"I got to feeling so good I stopped the thistle weed and that put me in trouble," Bones said. "If I just get on the weed regular, I don't believe I'll have any trouble."

Bones told Ben how badly he felt that he couldn't pay us back. Believe it or not, I was the one who said, "That's all right, Bones, pay us when you can." Tight-fisted, ungenerous me. The scorekeeper. I really did say that, startling myself.

"What about the Zodiac?" Ben said.

"I believe I'll take it down to Colorada with me and give my little girl a ride." He handed Ben the keys to the Triumph. "I cleaned her up real good and filled the gas tank," he said. Standing at the door, we watched Bones go. It was that same energetic walk I'd noticed when he had arrived.

"So much pain and so much will goes into that stride," I murmured to Ben, "and I really do think Bones will one day remember and pay us back."

Ben shrugged. "I never worry about that. Sometimes you have to help a guy out."

"And sometimes you can't help a guy out," I said. "All we did for Bones was buy him a lifestyle he couldn't handle."

"You just don't get it, do you, Carla? Bones is a man with a Zodiac." Ben scowled at me and stalked away.

Later, that afternoon, while Alex helped me wash windows, Ben's words kept coming back. Bones was a man with a Zodiac. Ben had suggested to Bones that he sell the ritzy craft and settle up. Yet he'd left Bones with the choice and Bones had taken what he needed. That fancy vessel no doubt served to salve his wounded ego. I could just see Bones running the Colorado River with his Mandy in her life vest squealing as she was pelted with spray. He'd leave the child memories of a glamorous dad who ran rivers and toured Europe and once owned a fishing trawler. Bones would not allow his child to see him as an ailing figure in a hospital bed.

A few weeks passed and I happened to meet Cap'n Jan, trawler owner, the old hulk now sporting an unusual paint job. Jan handed off pieces of our ailing Albin's diesel engine to Ben, who sat beside her, attending this brilliant mechanic, much as a nurse attends a physician.

Jan is, of course, the talk of the harbor, Jan and her plate-sized hands and her flamingo trawler with a candy striped awning and rows of seating on the ample deck. Cap'n Jan is offering lesbian cruises on her personal website, and why not? This is what the hands were saying on the dock. Who is going to argue with an amazon of a woman with an engineering degree? Ben was in awe of her, it was obvious, and Jan soon had me acting as her handmaiden, fetching pails of water to feed our parched diesel. She was wearing dangling earrings shaped like opened fans. The jewelry seemed to scream out, "Hey, look again! I'm no guy!"

Once the engine rumbled to life we all headed out for a trial run. Fumes from the surgery filled the tiny salon of the Albin. Jan and I lowered the top on our little deuce coupe of a vessel. I happened to ask Jan if she'd heard from Bones. A startled look crossed her plain face, regular enough that in the other gender she'd have made a handsome man. "Why yes," she murmured in her low-slung baritone: "Bones called me last night. He told me he's coming back sometime to take care of his obligations."

"How's his daughter?"

Jan shrugged, mowing a huge hand through a thatch of short hair. It was brownish gray underneath but blonde on top, and thick as a pelt. "Bones' ex-wife and her new husband left Colorado months ago. Bones called his ex's brother, who refused to tell him where they are."

I poured out my frustration to Cap'n Jan. How Bones refused to treat his illness. How he failed to take care of himself.

"I once had a friend with hepatitis C," Jan mused. A coffee cup she had been holding disappeared into her big hands, so that she appeared to be sipping coffee right out of a closed fist. "My friend was the same way. He'd have bouts of mania, wear himself out and then become totally lethargic and despondent. I think being somewhat manic/depressive is a part of the disease."

Jan's attention was drawn to the diesel then. She asked Ben to return to the dock and she soon had her head buried down beside the engine while Ben handed over wrenches as she asked for them. I paced the dock, waiting to fetch water, but my thoughts drifted back to Bones. Perhaps Cap'n Jan, doctor of diesels, was entirely correct and Bones was nothing other than the function of his own wasting.

Yet the Bones I now prefer to see is the one Ben had invested in: Bones as a minor angel in a Zodiac, pulling in some kids too weak to fight the current. Perhaps he's chopping scallions in someone's kitchen, breathing life into a party that's about to die. Just a small time angel, Bones is, doing the unsung and the unremarkable with a certain gusto and aplomb. Bones' exuberance gets the best of him, whereupon he falls into despair and has to pull himself back from the abyss. That he's able to do so is quite remarkable, or so it seems to me. I suppose you could say that Bones is simply a man without much of a liver. Then again, you would have to agree that there's not much wrong with his heart.

THE NIGHT DAD APPEARED IN THE WOODS

It was just another of my bright ideas; you can ask my brother Herb. Or Mom. How it all started was, I asked Herb to show us the trail through the woods. Mom and I had been taking our evening walks down the paved county road that runs past our farm. Just because it's a two-lane blacktop and not gravel, people drive like maniacs. They roar down a country road as if they are on the freeway, not out in the countryside with its amiably lethal roads. I was afraid that one of these days a car would hit us.

The only other place we can walk is up the old logging trail across from our driveway. It was where the Tjumslunds used to live. When they were in high school, my brother Herb and the two Tjumslund boys made a wonderful log cabin up there in the Tjumslunds' woods, but that was twenty-five years ago. The Ricters now own the Tjumslund place. As for the cabin the boys made, there's nothing left of it but a pile of logs falling away from one intact corner like oversized Lincoln Logs that some giant had cruelly kicked down.

I was uneasy whenever we took that old logging road because my mother said the Ricters are a little funny and keep pit bulls. But one evening we did trudge up that trail as far as the Ricters' driveway. The last time Dad managed to give Mom the slip, she said she'd called Mr. Ricter and asked him to look out for Dad. He hadn't bothered, she said. Several hours later, while the county search and rescue team mobilized, the sheriff drove up the Ricters' road himself and found Dad fallen down in a ditch.

These days Dad's well past running away; he can't even walk. Mom thought he wouldn't survive this last surgery, which is why she had asked Herb and me to come home. The mid-July heat was so oppressive it was usually late in the evening before we ventured out for our walks. While Mom and I stuck to the county roads, Herb and his wife Cecile had taken the trail along the edge of our woods, or so I found out. I knew their thinking, of course.

Herb and Cecile are athletes, the wiry types you see bicycling up mountain trails and rappelling off cliffs. They were training to join a mass climb of Mt. Adams over the Labor Day weekend. They didn't need Mom and me tagging along, slowing them down. But the three of us were leaving in the morning. Herb and Cecile were on their way back to Boise. They would drop me off at the Spokane airport where I could catch my flight back to Seatac. There I could connect with Island Air to my home on Orcas in the San Juan Islands. We were sluggish from a big dinner at the Mexican restaurant in town. It was still close to eighty degrees at seven p.m. I suppose Herb and Cecile figured it wouldn't hurt to accommodate the laggards on this last night. We would all tramp along together, as a gesture of family solidarity.

We started out past the old milk house, taking a long concrete bridge between the milk house and the loafing barn. Dad had constructed this walk so that his cows would have the best of care. He didn't want them to wade through muck between barns in the winter. I had forgotten about the walk. Herb had cleared off the weeds to reveal it and it is amazing what good shape it is in.

"I wish we could have a walking trail clear around the farm," I said to Herb. He responded with one of his droll little smiles and said nothing. Better than calling me stupid or a lunatic, I suppose. I realize now that Herb would have interpreted my comment as meaning that he should install such a trail. This would mean building new bridges across the two creeks, where the old structures had washed out. It would mean hacking a trail through the thistles that had gone to seed in the lower pastures, and chopping out the undergrowth that clogged the quarter section of woods.

Rather than responding directly, Herb simply stopped at the massive barn that gave off the walk, stuck his hands in his pockets and looked around. This was his subtle way of reminding me that the barns were to be his next project. We were standing in an enormous loafing barn where an entire herd of cattle could lounge in the winter. Just beyond it was a huge feeder shed. This comprised a barn big enough to hold some twenty tons of baled hay. Along one side of it ran a row of stanchions that could accommodate fifty cows at a feeding, a bovine dining hall of massive proportions.

Earlier in the day, Mom and I had walked through these same barns with Herb. The massive support posts were rotting at the bottom. Lyle Seidman and his son Burt had leased the upper pastures to grow hay and oats. They reinforced a few of the posts, but Mom was worried that a heavy snow could destroy one or the other of these buildings. Herb had told her not to worry and promised her that when he retired, a few years from now, he would finish repairing the barns himself. Herb reminded Mom that the barns had withstood the weather for the last thirty years. The support posts were milled from the nearly indestructible tamarack trees that Dad had harvested from the woods. So it was unlikely that the barns would topple anytime soon.

"Did you help Dad put up these sheds?" I asked Herb.

In response, my grizzled brother had simply rubbed his graying beard. Finally, he said, after what seemed way too long to consider such a simple question, "Well, not really. I was in grad school by the time he built these."

Just how Dad had managed to erect such massive structures virtually by himself was a mystery to me, and now, of course, it's too late to ask him. Yesterday we had all gone to town to see Dad. Mom wanted a family picture. Herb couldn't resist asking Dad if he knew who he was, even though I had warned him not to. You simply introduce yourself. Though of course, it does seem bizarre to say, "Hi Dad. I'm your son Herb."

Mom told Dad she wanted to take his picture with us. What set him off, we don't know, but he became enraged and called her a goddamned bitch and one of the attendants came over quickly and fumbled around taking the photo while Dad sat on the sofa, rigid as a mannequin, his face a bleak mask. Finally, I drew Cecile away from this ugly scene on the pretext of showing her the beautiful grounds and Dad's private room and I tried to explain away the hurt I read on her delicate face. When there are so many of us visiting at once, Dad gets confused, and when he gets confused, he lashes out.

Iron lady that she is, Mom kept her composure. We were halfway back to the farm when she blurted out, "It's been awhile since I've been sworn at."

Herb had cut a trail past the feeder shed adjacent to the woods. We were already on the overgrown woods path before we realized that it was rapidly getting dark. Herb assured us he knew the way, and so Mom and I tramped along behind Herb and Cecile, a quarter mile or so, until we came to the machinery graveyard. There was the hulk of an old truck. The enormous corkscrew shape of an old disk rose beside the truck and next to that stood a gothic structure I didn't recognize at all. The patina of rust on all these pieces was barely visible in the gathering dusk. But one of the contraptions we all recognized: Godzilla.

"Remember the hay trailer you and Dad built?" Mom said.

"Godzilla," I blurted, and we had a good laugh over the name.

Herb and Dad had built Godzilla one summer, a huge flat trailer with a ridiculously low suspension, barely a foot off the ground. Hay bales could be slipped onto the low, wide trailer bed as it slithered along between rows of baled hay, pulled by a tractor. Mom or I would drive. Dad, Herb, and a hired hand or two, would pick and stack the bales.

The beauty of Godzilla, aside from the name, was that bales could be stacked higher with fewer workers than on conventional trailers, with beds nearly shoulder high off the ground. Godzilla was a major labor saver, much easier on Dad's back, which was always going out. It wasn't long before Herb realized that if he could fashion a Godzilla, he could design a bridge or a building, and soon he was off to college to study engineering.

The machinery graveyard was located along the shoulder of the woods. To our left the rank, neglected pastures were dim in the graying light, but the fields of oats gleamed bronze in the setting sun. Yard lights were coming on in the magenta foothills beyond our valley, dozens of lights where once there had been three or four, back in the days when we knew every farmstead. All around us, the large parcels such as ours are being sold off by my parents' generation, broken up into ersatz farms maintained by people who keep a few horses or decorative creatures like llamas or emus, people who work for wages in town. Already our own farm has been whittled down by fifteen acres. A retired Army colonel is growing organic vegetables on the original farmstead. My grandparents' farmhouse is now the colonel's garden shed.

Why we didn't turn back at that point, I can't say, except that

Mom began to look for a road that Dad had cut through the woods. Cecile found a marker stake and I happened to look beyond it and could just make out that there was indeed a road cut into an aisle of trees, though overgrown by brambles and brush.

The four of us set off on the barely-visible road. Herb stomped down the thornier bushes under his hiking boots. Cecile held the branches out of our faces, and I came along slowly, shielding Mom from stray swipes of errant brambles. Mom, at eighty, managed to keep up. She was cheerfully riding me for getting us all into this. "Is this another of your bright ideas, Carla?"

Another iron stake was set into the trail ahead, and seeing it, I felt, was to take the measure of Dad. He must have installed the stakes at least twenty years ago. Someday, if the farm ever had to be divided off and sold, there was a certain way Dad wanted it to be done. Now that I was reminded of this, I realized what a shame it would be to do such a thing. I understood my mother's determination to cling to the farm though the fences fell down and the pastures went to seed and the barns toppled into heaps.

As Herb stomped at a snag ahead of us, a drumming of hooves arose somewhere through the dense timber. Deer: a whole herd of them, no doubt mightily confused to find their sanctuary invaded by humans at this time of the evening. But in the running sound I recalled Dad. Two summers ago he could still remember how to use his legs. Mom and I had walked with him as far as the machinery graveyard and then he had begun to walk faster until we had a hard time keeping up with him, and then he was running pell-mell and I was chasing him and I was thrilled. Dad was having fun. He was a free man enjoying a moment of clarity, of abandon; but then Dad fell on his face and cut himself on the brambles. It took nearly an hour before Mom convinced Dad that he could bend his legs and get up on his knees so that we could lift him up. Another of my better ideas that was: Get Dad on his feet. Take him for a walk. It's that simple. I had no idea that once he had started walking faster, he didn't know how to slow down.

We reached a grand stake that Mom said marked the heart of the farm, the exact center of the property. Dad had set the stake himself by taking compass readings off the neighbors' fence lines. A trail bore to the right off this, and so, instead of turning back, Herb decided we could forge ahead and make it back to the barns before it was too dark.

"We're coming to Ross's house," Cecile called over her shoulder.

"Ross had a playhouse?" I said to Mom. She nodded but went on, shunning this relic. Ross, our younger brother, had been an afterthought. He was born the year I graduated high school and so I knew little about him except what dismay his arrival caused Mom, then what a pet and a pleasure he'd become and how crushed my parents were when he was gone, lost to black ice on our blacktop road the night of his junior prom.

The playhouse had a real shingle roof and white lap siding. Through one window I could see a few stools and a camp stove. The ceiling was high enough that a child of eight or ten could stand up in it. The scale of it arrested me. Dad and Ross would have built it together. Most everything Mom and Dad had done for their children was bigger than life. When Herb was growing up, boys played cowboy and Herb got a set of hand-made chaps, sewn from real leather with the fur still on it, and trimmed with real Mexican silver doodads, the kind the bronco riders favored when they rode the bucking horses at the rodeo. My own earliest memory of any toy was of a giant teddy bear which stood twice as tall in my crib as I did, and Dad's impish expression as he propped the towering straw bear in its striped overalls in the corner of my bed.

The white siding on the playhouse turned gray and the shingle roof receded into the sullying dark. Ahead, I could make out the rest of the family by the sounds of brush mashing underfoot, Cecile's throaty giggle, and the beacon of Mom's silver hair. Our procession ended at the remains of the sawmill Dad built so that he could harvest the timber and plane it into the lumber that went into the building of his huge sheds. I could just make out the circle of a saw blade taller than I was and the rails of the sled that bore the logs to the blade.

There was scant light left, a gloom through which to limn a man of ambitious ideas, of expansive thoughts. In the dark, we kept to the faint trail marked here and there with iron stakes. Shards of the remaining daylight flashed among the tall pines as we picked our way back to the edge of the trail that returned us to our starting point in front of Dad's enormous barns. Dad had set out the trail and the markers a score of years ago. Dad, a man of genius he'd been, a builder of outsized proportions, a thinker. I wondered if he had had then any inkling whatever of his coming decline. Had he laid out this final monument to himself in the woods, this trail to guide us back in some way to all that he had been?

But as I say, it is now too late to ask him. Dad simply says yes to everything, and perhaps to wonder such a thing is just another of my bright ideas.

Yes.

MISS ARCADIA MISSES HIGH SCHOOL

A stunning red car said it all. It cruised into the circular drive just as Carla (Hughes) Bridges rang the doorbell of Judy (Priest) Steadman's grand house. The car was an antique something-or-other. Carla wasn't up on her cars but anyone could see that this was a gem. Such wheels belonged in the garage of a rock star or a dotcom millionaire. Such transportation suggested that someone in her high school class had prospered. Carla had noticed the red beauty earlier. It had been the most gleaming entry among the vintage autos in this morning's Pioneer Days Parade.

It was clear also that Judy Steadman had done well for herself by the standards of a Columbia Gorge town like Arcadia, Washington. This small town had a long and prosperous history as a ranching and mining center and was the Simcoe County seat. However, the City of Arcadia itself had become an antique, sporting fourteen Victorian era homes on the National Historic Register. Trouble was, the business district was moribund, comprised of second hand stores and consignment shops, and the location of Judy Steadman's home was even further down the economic ladder.

Judy Steadman's current address was in the nearby enclave of Antler. This had caused Carla some concern. Antler had never been a viable community. Antler consisted of a tavern and some rundown trailer parks along the Simcoe River. For as long as Carla could remember, Arcadia residents had dismissed Antler. To get to Judy's, Carla had turned off the highway north of Arcadia, passed the ramshackle Antler Tavern, "home of the famous Antler burger," crossed the railroad tracks and tunneled along through tall, pencil-straight pines. As Carla arrived at Judy's woodsy residence, she revised her estimate of Antler upwards. There were several fancy new homes in Judy's neighborhood, hidden away from the squalor of the town. Judging by the array of pickups, RVs, SUVs, 4x4s, and other assorted chrome gleaming along a circular drive, Carla knew she had arrived at her intended destination—the reunion party for the Arcadia High School Class of '65.

Judy Steadman's farmhouse sat in acres of perfect lawn, was bordered in dense floral beds and manicured shrubbery and was dotted with old farm implements enameled in spiffy colors. Washtubs and antique kitchen appliances served as flowerpots. A purple clematis trailed off the wringer of an old washing machine. The latest in high-powered petunias, a variety known as "the wave," billowed from the gaping door of an acid green cast iron stove.

There was a long pause after Carla rang Judy's bell, which she interpreted as a slight she was due. After all, she had declined to ride on the "class of '65" float in the Pioneer Days parade earlier in the day. Carla had watched from the sidelines, joking with her mother and uncles with whom she had watched the parade. She told them she had wanted to ride the "Class of `85" float instead, but that they wouldn't let her on.

Carla had scrutinized the very latest Miss Arcadia, however, taking note of this year's style of wave. The latest Miss Arcadia swept her arm through a languid, figure eight motion, a delicate finger painting of the air. In Carla's day, the approved wave had been a more rigid windshield wiper motion, elbow fixed, fingers closed, pledge-allegiance style. This later became known as "the Princess Di wave." Due to the extremely chilly weather, this latest Miss Arcadia in her strapless gown smiled gamely through blue lips. Though the weather had been beautiful for a week, a chilling downpour had started in the half hour before the Arcadia Days Parade, dampening the festivities.

The freezing shower and glowering clouds brought back to Carla memories of her own turn as Miss Arcadia, '65, where the rides on the floats were scalding or freezing by turns. The lilacs had refused to bloom for the Lilac Festival in Spokane. Carla's long gloves had been frozen to her arms. Her smile had wobbled the entire length of the grand parade due to the chattering of her teeth. In thirty-five years, the hazards of being named a "Miss Arcadia" had not abated.

The weather had not cleared until now, two hours after the

parade. Carla, who had spent nearly a decade in Hawaii, could no longer tolerate the chills of her native Pacific Northwest, and had held off her arrival at Judy's garden party until the sun came out. Eventually Judy arrived at the door and swept Carla into her ample arms, even as she scolded her for ignoring previous queries into her whereabouts for the last three decades. Carla laid this off to the fact that she had been in New York, Washington, D.C., Jamaica, Australia, Maui, or the San Juan Islands. What Carla could not admit to Judy was that she had exiled herself from her own graduating class.

By her own standards, Carla's behavior had been inexcusable. Her imperfection had shown in her treatment of her first major boyfriend Jace Roberts in her senior year. The whole town of Arcadia had to have known she was not the queen they had elected. Carla and her husband Ben had returned to live in Washington State, however. After Ben retired, they had moved to their Orcas Island summer place in Ben's beloved San Juan Islands. Meanwhile, Carla visited Arcadia frequently to help her mother look after her ailing father. When Judy's invitation to the Class of '65 Reunion came along, to be held in conjunction with Arcadia's Pioneer Days, Carla decided she ought to face up to the havoc she had created so many years ago.

While looking around for Jace Roberts, to whom she owed an apology, one of the tall, balding males stepped out of a cluster of similarly tonsured men and kissed her on the cheek. It was Steve Hoines. Steve was now much more animated than he had been in high school. Back then he had been the science fair nerd. It wasn't long before he let Carla know that the glamorous red car she had seen in the driveway was his, a 1940 four-door Olds Street Rod, to be precise. Steve said he and his wife spent their time going to car shows.

Carla laughed with Steve about how mechanized the Pioneer Days parade had become. It was now a glorified car show. There had been dozens of antique cars, including Steve's Olds, a slew of restored Ford Mustangs, plus six or eight of those high-wheeled monsters that wallowed in mud pits. The monsters rode fancy trailers, towed by enormous pickup trucks. The drivers of these elaborate trucks revved their engines every quarter mile or so to perfume the crowds with gasoline stench.

"Why were the mud buggies all on trailers?" Carla said.

"They aren't road worthy. Their suspensions are way too wide,"

Steve said.

There were few floats of the tissue-stuffed-in-chicken-wire type. This was due to the lack of housewives with the energy to do the work. These days the ladies mostly had careers. The wealthy baby boomers like Hoines, who had retired from the government with a good pension, preferred to invest their creative energies in glamorous, wheeled trophies that would no doubt bring in a pot of money if they ever went to auction. Or was it that Carla's generation, among the earliest of the Boomers, could not grow up? They had to have their fancy wheels.

Carla's old girlfriends were off in their usual clique. All of them—Marcy, Dale, Toni, and Patty—were still married to their high school sweethearts. And yes, Holly Roberts was there, Jace's wife. Holly was not to be missed. She'd let her thick hair grow white, and it was totally stunning with her beautiful skin and big gray eyes, glistening, driftwood eyes, and she was as slender as she ever was. All of them were cordial and seemed interested in how Carla had moved around, though of course, they all had large traditional weddings to which, in the year after graduation, Carla had not been invited.

Carla, who had had her daughters late in life, didn't stick around when her old friends got out their pictures of their grandchildren. Instead she was taken up by all the shy, stray males of old who now had grand tales to tell. Clark Madden, still tall and pale with a beaky nose and a thick, swallowed way of speaking, regaled her with his Florida story: how he and his buddies had wrestled a ten-foot gator into the office of the commanding officer of their platoon, how nobody would own up to the prank, how they'd been run for miles, and still nobody would come forward, and how he'd never been accorded proper credit for inventing the prank. Everyone thought it was so funny they all stole a piece of the action.

The buffet lunch was about to be served and so Carla headed for the serving line, turned toward the party on her elbow and there he was: Jace Roberts.

"Carla," he said. "I wouldn't have recognized you."

"Well Jaaa-ce," she said, and they touched cheeks. Jace, never awfully tall, was stooped now, scarcely taller than Carla. Slightly balding, but still Jace with his dark, rich coloring and enormous black eyes dominating a compact face. Jace looked like that actor. The one married to Gena Rowlands. Oh. What was his name?

If Carla had followed the plan that all her girlfriends had, she'd have married Jace right out of high school. Right after he'd done his tour in Viet Nam. But as it happened, after Jace had left, Carla had gone on to being just as much in love with Alan Trupin who was a scholar, athlete, musician, and the valedictorian of his class, '62.

And yet Carla had gone on writing to Jace all along, mentioning everything about Arcadia except her attachment to Alan. It was stupid. It was unconscionable. But somehow Carla couldn't bear to have Jace think she was less than perfect, especially when all the guys in his platoon were getting their Dear John letters. Or else stepping on land mines and getting killed. Somehow, at the back of Carla's mind, she could not place herself among lesser women. The Miss Arcadia banner hung heavily around her neck. She had to keep up standards.

Jace mustered out six weeks early to surprise Carla and she, out of shock, rejected him on the spot. It sent him spiraling into a three-day drunk. Carla's close friend, Holly, now of the beautiful white hair, spent so much time comforting Jace that she broke up with her own boyfriend, Donny Holloway, whom she had been dating for the same two years that Carla had been going with Alan Trupin. Jace and Holly quickly became the power couple. Theirs was the hottest romance in town.

Carla, who had come to the reunion to apologize to Jace, was now tongue-tied in the face of his expansiveness. Jace said he owned a chain of western outfitter stores and a stable of quarter horses in Wyoming.

"I had a stroke eighteen months ago," Jace was saying. "Holly pulled me through. She got me right into the emergency room and the damage was minimal. It was a killer on the memory, though. Customers I've had for twenty years will say hello and I'll have no idea who they are."

"Well I'm flattered that you remembered me," Carla said and slipped away. She had not brought up to this prosperous and happy man the fact that she had been a painful episode in his life. Somehow the simple fact of seeing Jace again had allowed Carla to absolve herself. Jace said he had three sons and two daughters, all of them involved in the family businesses, whereas Carla had hopped from coast to coast and in and out of several marriages.

Though Carla had intended that her visit to this reunion be an act of contrition, she found herself listening instead to Eddie Donovan blurt out over lunch that the high point of his Arcadia career was that he was accused of a kidnapping. Carla was aghast. Eddie Donovan had retired as an Air Force Colonel. Eddie was a decorated war hero with forty missions over Viet Nam. They had met once out of high school, in human phys class at the U in Seattle, before Carla headed off for Washington, D.C. to work as a government intern. Eddie had rescued Carla from dissecting frogs when she volunteered to write all their lab reports.

Carla sat next to Eddie, leaning close to study him. Eddie seriously had not changed. Not a wrinkle. He still wore a crew cut and had no bald spot. He still squinted out of his left eye and spoke with the same sardonic tone.

"Darren Campbell, Rocky Winthrop, and I went cruising down Main in Darren's folks' black Chrysler. We were riding past The Hut," Eddie said, sounding like some anchorman reading a news story about someone else entirely.

"The old tavern?"

"That's right. Out of the alley comes the kid that lived behind it. Darren might have spun a little gravel on him. This little kid gives us the finger, and after all, we were seniors. We were having none of that. Darren jumps out of the car. The kid took off down the alley but Darren nailed him in ten yards."

"Nobody could outrun Darren Campbell," Carla hooted to the reserved blonde sitting beside Eddie. His wife? Carla guessed. Eddie hadn't introduced her.

"Darren Campbell, fastest man in the State," Eddie said to the blonde, "three times champion in the sprint."

The blonde said nothing. Perhaps this confession was something she had not heard? Or perhaps she thought it was best this never be told?

"We threw the kid in the backseat and took off for the airport," Eddie said. "We tied him up to the gate. Then we drove off. We hid behind a hangar with the lights off and let the kid chill for about fifteen minutes. Then we went back and untied him and took him home."

"Good Lord," Carla said. Today such a story would have been on the news. It had overtones of that terrible story of that gay kid tied to a fence and murdered. There would have been lawsuits and no end of uproar, and here was a story Carla was hearing for the first time. It was as if she had never gone to Arcadia High. The amazing part was, this was Eddie talking. Eddie Donovan had lettered in everything.

"Next day we are all in study hall and we get this command to go see Angle."

"No," Carla said.

"So the little kid was late to dinner and he caught it from his folks. What did he have to offer in the way of an excuse? 'Sorry Mom, I got kidnapped.'"

"Did they put you in juvenile?" Carla said.

"We paid our dues," Eddie said, adding, "Hey, these ribs aren't bad," and he attacked his lunch.

Carla, scooping up fruit salad, thought of the two boys Eddie had been with. Darren Campbell, of all people. Had Darren been saved by his standing as the school's most notable athlete? By his State record in the ten meter dash?

As for Rocky Winthrop, he had arrived in their sophomore year. Rocky was Mr. Cool. Rocky Winthrop had been the king of the Junior Prom. Now he was on Judy Priest's missing-in-action reports. He had disappeared from notice and nobody had heard from him. Was it possible that Rocky, like Carla, had exiled himself? Was it possible that Rocky, punishing himself for his transgression, could not face coming back to Arcadia and owning up to a kidnapping?

As Carla turned away bearing a piece of the obligatory class cake stenciled with a load of grads hanging out of a Mustang, she found herself in the path of a pudgy man with an enormous handlebar moustache.

"Carla!" he blurted. "My God. You look fantastic. I mean, weren't you kind of fat in high school?"

Carla sidled closer, peering into a pair of tawny eyes. She knew who it was. You had to study the eyes. The layers of wrinkles, weathered skin and pouchy deposits around the edges seemed like a disguise applied by the movie department.

"Todd Fralik," she said. They embraced and Todd whirled her around, cake and all. Todd Fralik had been stationed in the Navy at Norfolk while Carla was at Georgetown in Washington, D.C. He had written her a letter, telling her how smart she was to get away from Arcadia, suggesting they get together. She had ignored him. She was dating an important aide to Senator Jackson at the time.

Now Todd reminisced about how he dated every girl in the class. "I took you out," he said to Carla. She didn't recall that, either.

Todd, ever the rebel, was telling her how it was illegal for the IRS to collect taxes. How she could sue.

"After you," Carla said.

"I did. I took my case to the Supreme Court. I lost."

Todd, one of the class grads who had returned to live in Arcadia after retiring from the military, was helping Judy Priest host the event. Judy called Todd up to the back porch that doubled as a stage.

On the porch, Todd strutted back and forth, grooming his moustache with a forefinger. "And now it's time for the Unsolved Mysteries of the class of '65." He unrolled a long scroll and got a big laugh.

"Who was the culprit who threw a bunch of chickens in the gym the night of the sock hop?"

"I don't exactly know," Clark Madden said, the alligator prankster. "However, as you may remember, I didn't graduate with the class. I was asked to leave school."

Clark took a bow to a round of applause.

"Next mystery," Todd said. "Does anybody know why Angle got a bee in his bonnet and cancelled the Junior Hop?"

Nobody responded.

"I never did figure that one out," Todd said.

"Angle was a communist," someone called, a remark which got howls. In truth, of course, Mr. Angle was anything but. At the beginning of their senior year, the hatchet-faced principal had gone to some national symposium, called the entire student body into a special meeting in the gym and ranted for an hour about how he was going to return the school to Basic American Values.

"It was the Red Scare," someone else suggested.

"Mr. Angle was a hero in his own mind, and so I never did understand why he took so unkindly to the incident where someone installed the scooter he rode to school in the trophy case," Todd said. He brushed his fingers across his paintbrush moustache.

The fact that the principal was still known as "Angle" after forty years brought back to Carla the fact that the school board ousted Mr. Angle for alleged corporal punishment.

Carla had been one of Mr. Angle's few defenders. She had worked in the office. She thought the principal quietly arranged to help the poor kids without any fanfare. She never did know for certain whether Mr. Angle arranged for Billy Hardin to have all his rotten teeth pulled and replaced with dentures, but in her own mind Carla had been certain of this at the time.

"When Angle summarily cancelled the Junior Hop, that was the beginning of the end," Todd said. "I got my parents to lease the grange hall. We arranged for chaperones and when Angle turned up, the parents who were there told him he wasn't welcome."

This was news to Carla. She couldn't remember the hop in the Grange Hall. Carla had prided herself on attending every single dance. Had she been deliberately excluded by the Angle-haters at the time? Or was she left out because Jace and Holly were the star attraction?

Todd quieted his audience with a new announcement. "There were harrowing times in the Angle Regime when certain valorous acts went unnoticed. For instance, the outstanding work of Holly Roberts and the decorating committee for the Senior Prom. Holly, come on up here. Take a bow."

A blushing Holly took the stage, stepping nervously in a kind of swaying box step. She'd always done it, even when they had been in the senior play together. Carla had made an entry half a scene early, leaving Holly to figure out how to get off stage. Had this been an unconscious sabotage on Carla's part?

"Spring of '65 was a total disaster," Holly began. "Our theme was Spring Flowers. There wasn't a blossom to be had in Arcadia. The only flowers in bloom in the eastern half of the state were seventy miles away—on Spokane's South Hill."

Holly's deep alto voice dropped to its most intimate level. "So an ad hoc committee was formed, the Flower Posse. We met for fuel at Zip's, and stormed the South Hill after midnight.

"My shoes sank to the ankles in one yard. Our lookouts whistled. Somebody was coming. We had to get out of there fast. I had to step right out of my Keds and leave them behind in the muck. Next morning we made the paper. There was an article about vandalism on the South Hill."

As applause broke out, Holly let rip a few bars of the Arcadia Fight Song, which the graying classmates bellowed out with tears in their eyes. Carla could not sing for the remorse she felt. Yes, she'd been Miss Arcadia. She'd won a few scholarships and had one of the longest lists of accomplishments in the yearbook. But as she looked around at the cheering grads, it was only to see that her classmates had known much more about high school than she had ever known. Or ever would.

A MOUNTAINDALE WEDDING

Why I was desperate to catch me a big sturgeon? It was because Lara had her heart set on one grand wedding dress. She saw it on the cover of *Bride's Magazine*. Lara never bothered me about it, of course. I am crazy in love with Lara. I'd do anything to please her, but it's hard to do for the sweetest, most soft-spoken woman you can imagine. To this day I can't get Lara to choose the place I take her of a Saturday night. I decide whether it'll be Mexican, Chinese, or pizza. I never would have heard a word about the wedding dress at all except I overheard Lara pleading for it with her daddy.

I'd been pouring cement out to Uncle Elmer Bingin's and got home early. Lara was on the phone with her old man. I kissed her on that ticklish place on her neck and her shoulders squinched. I heard her go on about the train, the satin, the lace, and the crystal beads. It was the price tag got my attention: Six hundred dollars.

"But Daddy. You told me you'd pay for the wedding," Lara said, her back to me, but her sad look reflected back at me in the kitchen window. There was a silence while Lara took in what was said. She kept her face to the window as she hung up, hiding her disappointment.

I poured a little of my Red Dog into a glass for her and sat down at the kitchen table. Lara slumped across from me and smiled a smaller than usual smile. Then she took a larger than usual swallow of beer, Lara with her valentine face, her eyes blue as the foothills at sunset, and Miss Virtue herself. She won't touch pot, won't smoke, hates partying. Lara might sip a beer when we're home for an evening. That's it.

"The old man's backing down?"

"Daddy says nine hundred for the whole wedding." Not a tinge of anger in her tone.

"That old skinflint," I said, his own words in my ears: "I'll pay for the wedding, Donny Ray. Anything for my girl." This made perfect sense to me. Lara's the prettiest of the Byers girls. Never in trouble. Not one shoplifting charge. Never a speeding ticket. Never skipped school a day in her life. Never got pregnant her senior year. Lara didn't have to get married. No sir. Lara deserved a fine wedding, never mind her intended happens to be a man with a checkered past.

"Daddy's retired. A man on a pension," Lara said, smiling little. She won't hear a bad word against that bastard. Never paid a nickel in child support and was drunk the night of Lara's high school graduation. Roberta herself told me this. Roberta is Lara's mother. But hey, Roberta herself was probably stoned.

"Mama told me to try this consignment shop in Portland where doctors' wives sell clothes they wear one time," Lara said. This was the story of Lara's life. She couldn't expect to get what she wanted.

"Put that dress on layaway, darlin'. I'll figure a way pay for it. I don't want you getting married to me in a used dress. A used husband's bad enough." I took her palm and kissed it along the lifeline, right up to the pulse beating in her wrist. I adore that girl. If Lara hadn't sat behind me come the day of my trial looking serene and confident in my basic decency and good intentions, I might still be off on my long vacation at taxpayer's expense.

Lara and I were fated. I believe that. We met on the courthouse steps the day of my arraignment, the first Monday in May that was, year before last. I looked good in my church suit, all my jailhouse tattoos covered up. Otherwise, I don't know as Lara would have had the gumption to blurt out how she was in love with me and had been ever since she was thirteen. She'd seen me and my cousins running our hogs down the old loops by the Columbia River, test roads they built back when they said no highways could be built in the Columbia Gorge.

I once gave Lara a ride on my Harley and was polite to her; or so she said. I don't recall the incident. I suspect I was drunk at the time. The way we boys ran those loops, I don't know why we're alive. We were the wild and dangerous Carter cousins and I was head of the pack. We never lacked for women. I would never of given a skinny twerp like Lara Byers a second glance.

Lara and I set our wedding date come our two-year anniversary of that day in May, our way of putting a bad time behind us. The white lilacs was sending out their perfume outside the courthouse windows, and so we'll have the Mountaindale Grange Hall decked with white lilacs for our wedding.

Funny how love can blossom out of trouble. I can't say as we'd have met again at all, except the judge heard my not-guilty plea on the exact same day Lara's mama Roberta got probation on her third pot offense.

They say marijuana ain't damaging, not addictive, but then there's Lara's mom. Roberta's a flower child who never blossomed. Never recovered from her camp-follower days with the Grateful Dead. Lara humors Roberta. Lara's the mother as far as I can see, while Roberta never matured past the bud.

In my case, Mama had warned me time and again about my drinking and my temper. She raised hell every time I got nailed with another drunk and disorderly. On the other hand Mama knew what went on between me and my ex. Mama put up my bond. My attorney got my case delayed twice. Lara and I had six months together before my case come to trial.

When that dark October day came round, Lara sat there serenely while that bitch prosecutor waved those photos of my ex-wife Trisha, with purple bruises on her neck and two black eyes. Them pictures did me in. I could feel them jury ladies giving me the squinty eye.

The judge wouldn't allow nothing into evidence about Trisha being known as "Tricks" to every bar fly in Mountaindale. It cut no ice that I'd worked the wheat harvest in blistering heat. I stopped at the Frontier Inn for a cool one. I admitted right there in court that I lingered on and got home late. But Trish was gone. That girl had gone out on one of her dates leaving our two young daughters asleep in the house. It was bad enough that Trish stepped out on me, but neglecting the children was more than I could take.

I have a drinking problem, still do. I admitted it in court. I went to rehab and took anger management before my case come up, but there you go. Take an eighteen-month vacation in the state facilities, the judge said.

I looked back at Lara, my eyes all teary. She smiled and held up her amethyst ring and stroked it with her fingers. We'd been engaged since the middle of July. I will never forget that scorching summer weekend I gave Lara the amethyst ring with diamond chips around it, tied up in a velvet box.

Just like the dress, I had to learn about the ring by accident. I overheard Lara telling her baby half-sister, Josey. It was the hottest Fourth of July weekend on record in Mountaindale. No cooling wind come off the Cayuse Hills. I'd finished a roofing job and was home by noon so we could take the kids to the parade. Josey sat chillin' in her wet bathing suit, dripping into Lara's lap. They was watching the Home Shopping Network. These rings with the amethyst stones came on. Lara told Josey how she loved them amethysts, the same purple of our woods lilies, the mariposas. I called up Mama right then. I asked Mama to call Home Shopping and order an amethyst ring for Lara on the spot, seeing as how quantities was limited.

The year of my vacation in the state facilities, that whole dismal time, we wrote back and forth about the wedding. I was released in November, a week before Thanksgiving. Six months was knocked off my time for good behavior. We set the wedding date for the first week in May, two years from the day of our courthouse meeting.

So here we are, near the end of January, most of the plans is complete. The families have been invited. The wedding's to be enormous. Lara's from Witnesses on her mother's side. Our clan being Adventists, we got people coming from here to Texas.

Problem from the start was the Witnesses wouldn't set foot in no church. Now Lara and me, we compromised on our religion. We go to the community service where there's no sermon. All the readings come straight from the Bible. No preacher gives out false doctrine. Still this is too much church for the Witnesses among us. Lara didn't complain when we compromised some more and booked our wedding at the Mountaindale Grange.

The Grange ladies are doing the dinner. No finer country cooking is to be had in this nation. Fried chicken and prime rib. Haunch of elk and poached venison—and I'm not talking about the style of cooking, neither. I admit I took out an extra deer or two. Wouldn't have been out of season but for bad luck. This country's so overrun with deer that hell's bells—the government rightly should give me a couple of medals for losing them two.

You have to hang venison the way Daddy taught, then lard them roasts with bacon fat. Wasn't Daddy that strung the carcasses up in the garage. Let me be clear on that. Daddy don't dare pick up a rifle and hunt another lick. He's subject to lie detector tests until the end of his probation. Daddy says he don't want to take another state holiday over a missing deer. Daddy don't care for state accommodations and since I've been there myself, I can't say I blame him.

About that wedding dress, Mama fussed. When I stopped by Mama's shop to tell her, she stopped in the middle of a comb-out and poked the rattail end of the comb at me. "Lot of money for a dress, Donny Ray Carter. Lot of dress for a grange wedding."

"Cripes, Mama. Don't you think Lara deserves it?"

"Lara's the best thing that ever happened to you, son, never mind she ain't Adventist." Mama curled this old lady's gray locks over her finger. She set that curl to the lady's head with the care she takes to set frosted roses on the cakes she bakes. For the wedding, Mama's doing the finest cake Mountaindale has ever seen.

"Don't look to me on the dress, Donny Ray," Mama said. "You still owe me a sum on the ring. Plus interest."

"I wasn't asking, Mama."

"Of course not. You never was any genius, Donny Ray, but you do show some sense. At least now and then."

At first Mama was not happy when we moved in together in August, right after we got engaged. Lara was barely eighteen and I was on the wrong side of thirty, facing the possibility of a long vacation at taxpayer expense. Plus, I got my three kids. Lara's but five years older than Jed my boy that moved in with me. The way my ex Trish carries on with the biggest drug dealer between Bend and Yakima, I do expect I'll get custody of my two girls one day. Melody is six and Andrea is eight.

"Lara's a child, Donny Ray," Mama'd say. "Suppose you get convicted? How could Lara pay the rent? How would Lara cope with your three kids?"

Didn't matter none, I'd tell Mama. We both love kids. Between Lara and me we got five youngsters to look after. Half the time Lara's in charge of her sister Josey and Josey's older half- sister Trina. Half the time her Mama Roberta is zoned out, sprinkling daisies somewhere inside her head.

Elmer Bingin, being my uncle by marriage, he and Aunt Stella, they are invited to the wedding. Aunt Stella asked how the plans was coming. I told her about how I was going to spring for the fine wedding dress. We were having lunch, Stella's pot roast. I was pouring cement for Uncle Elmer's new horse barn. The winter was warm, the ground wasn't frozen. It was okay to pour. Elmer didn't say much, just drew on his corncob pipe and looked wise. Elmer might look like a white-haired troll with a thick beard and a light bulb for a nose, but he's one of the most respected ranchers in the valley. First he raised prized beef, then champion quarter horses and now his thoroughbreds have won some races.

Come quitting time, Uncle Elmer pulled me aside. Said he had some big cheeses coming from the horsemen's association. Wanted Aunt Stella to make her famous deep-fried sturgeon. I knew right then what Uncle needed from me. Rancher he might be but Elmer never was no fisherman. What Elmer wanted was for me and Daddy to go after the sturgeon.

"Winter season's open," I said. "Might be doable. How much sturgeon you talking?"

"Two hundred pounds, maybe three."

 "Consider it done, Uncle Elmer."

"Course I'll pay you." Elmer lit his pipe.

"I couldn't take a thing for it."

"What say we trade for a wedding dress?" The smoke he exhaled smelled like wet sawdust.

"Could do, sir."

"It'll be a gift."

"Whatever you say, Uncle."

That's Uncle Elmer for you. I was to earn our wedding gift, but that's how Uncle got where he is today. As for me, I was thrilled. I'll do anything for Lara.

Except for bad weather, we'd of had sturgeon in Elmer's fridge the next afternoon. A chill set in and hung on. Nasty weather, the sturgeon won't bite, but let me tell you, them fish are out there. The Columbia River is the finest sturgeon fishery in this nation. That's what they say. Daddy and I got our heavy tackle ready and dipped smelt for bait.

By the time the weather cleared Uncle Elmer was anxious. He had his dinner coming in three days' time. I worked on Elmer's barn in the morning. Daddy picked me up from the job in the early afternoon. He was towing his little cabin cruiser behind his pickup.

We offloaded at the ramp down by White Salmon and headed into the Columbia. We went for a certain hole, well clear of the spillway of the Bonneville Dam. A spit there forks into the River and the water pools behind it. Sturgeon's bottom feeders. You have to find a place where the bait settles into crannies. The fish know to swim along and suck the bait into their gill rakers.

A sturgeon's got no teeth where teeth ought to be. The teeth are on its back, these snags called scutes, you see. A sturgeon is one of God's ancient creations. Maybe He didn't quite have the design to His liking. This explains how the good Lord could create anything so ugly as a sturgeon. Might be the Lord has a reason a big sturgeon runs close on to an orca whale in size. Such a fish puts the mortal fear in the likes of puny fishermen like me.

Daddy and I had Roll Mop pickled herring with us; too gourmet for the population, I guess. When we fish together, Daddy always brings out the Roll Mop. I had Roll Mop on the line the time a sturgeon pulled me right out of the boat. I was eight, maybe nine. That fish came on with a real light bite. I yanked back on the line and it was splish splash I was taking a bath just like they say in that old song.

"First I seen you, then you was gone." Daddy sat in the boat playing his line, howling at that story like he does, till he has to wipe tears from his eyes.

"I hung on, Daddy. I landed that fish."

"You sure did, Donny Ray. Proved yourself a fisherman right then."

We switched to some shad that Daddy had left over in the freezer, hoping them sturgeon wouldn't be reading no calendars. It's too early for shad in its natural state but later, in the spring, the runs of shad on the upper river draw swarms of sturgeon from the lower pools behind the dams. The shad didn't do it so we tried our fresh smelt. Late in the afternoon a wind came up and bit us good. We took turns on the deck. One or other of us went below to warm up by the propane heater and nip at the applejack.

We'd anchored on a buoy to keep the boat from crowding the spillway. The boat was drifting with the current. I saw what might have been a bite. If the bait's in a crag, the fish might take it and you can't feel a nibble. I took the rod just in case. The next bite was no maybe. I yelled for Daddy to come on up and take over the boat. I hauled back to set the hook; the rod bowed and I knew I had a big one, the right size and then some. If I could only land it, Lara had her wedding dress.

Daddy cut us loose from the buoy. He was hard on the wheel, fighting to keep us from running aground. "Damn. Would you look at that?" he said as the sturgeon broke the surface, bone-white against a dying day. It leaped up tail high, looking half as big as the boat to say the least; it sounded and come up again, long as I was tall, looking meaty enough to feed all them horse breeders and maybe even their thoroughbreds.

This went on for three or four leaps. Sturgeon's feisty. They'll put up a real fight and this was one stubborn fish. It sounded and leaped, leaped and sounded, and like to of dragged us over that dam. Daddy played the boat just right, letting the sturgeon have room to run. When he felt the fish resting he'd back the boat off to keep up the tension and I'd reel hard.

The sun sank over the bare ridge above the Columbia and I was sick and tired of hauling on the line. My arms went rubbery. My back screamed. My legs was gone, it seemed. Came one mighty leap and fish sighed and settled down. I whooped and hollered, praised sweet Jesus that the battle was done. Daddy put us back on the anchor buoy and got out the lasso line.

There's nothing sleek and silvery about a sturgeon. They's rough as gators, studded with rows of spikes and they can twist around and snap your wrist in nothing flat. That's why we lassoed this one from the tail end. We pulled the fish alongside the boat and rolled her on her back to calm her down. I snugged the line around her middle. Daddy cut the hook out of her gill raker and commenced to saw at the lasso line.

"What the hell, old man?"

"Look for yourself, son. She's over limit. Seventy inches and then some."

"Not a fin over sixty."

"Just ain't so, Donny. We got to release her."

"This is a hardship catch."

Daddy's lip curled. "Hardship? A fish fry for a passel of horse breeders? The judge would laugh in your face."

"Uncle Elmer's counting on me and so's Lara. Girl's got to have her wedding dress."

Daddy's lip twisted toward his squinty eye. "We're skating on the edge, son. Done my last night in the pokey. If a trip to the pen don't teach you nothing—"

"You're shivering sir. I believe you need to get below. Take another shot of applejack."

"I ain't having no part of this," the old man muttered.

"Agreed."

When I checked the fish, she lay on her back, nice and quiet. Trouble was, we still had a good two hours' daylight. No time to dress out a sturgeon that might be a bit over limit. Also, there was a problem with the lasso line. Daddy hanked it on a cleat on the stern. It wasn't near long enough for what I had in mind. There was no spare line in the hatches, neither. I went to the bow and hacked the bow line right off the boat. Too bad Daddy saw that from below. By the time I was back on the stern, he'd poked his head up through the cabin hatch.

"What the hell you think you're doing, Donny Ray?"

"There's a fray in the bow line. I'll buy you a new one."

Daddy turned around and went below, his shoulders hunched, and that was the last thing he said to me for the rest of the trip.

I hitched the bow line from the boat to the end of the lasso around the fish, to make a nice long leader. I eased the boat over to the lowest part of the bank, towing the fish alongside. I nosed the bow ashore, hopped out, and tied the line to the biggest tree on the bank. Before I released the fish from the cleat on the boat, I rolled her upright gently, and pitched the line into the water as far from the boat as I could. The sturgeon was still exhausted and didn't so much as switch her tail as she nosed around the puddle of line. She hadn't figured out she was tied to a tree. I eased the boat back into the current, taking care not to snag my sturgeon's leash in the prop.

We had scant light to get back to the boat launch. Our trailer was the last one in the parking lot. Galen Winthrop, the fish and game warden, drove in as we pulled out. Galen, he looks like a preacher with those short black whiskers from ear to ear and his big round paunch. He talks like a preacher as well, a preacher from the wildlife synod. Daddy rolled down the window and passed the time.

Galen asked us how the fishing was; Daddy said we took no keepers. Galen waved us on.

"It must be his supper time or he'd have checked our licenses," I said. Daddy shook his head and worked the plug of tobacco in his jaw. I checked the rearview mirror. Galen turned 14-West toward White Salmon. We headed 14-East toward the Mountaindale turnoff.

Daddy grunted when he dropped me off. He didn't invite me to stop over for supper, neither, but I'm used to that. His new wife, she's a Witness so firm in her faith that I don't quite meet up to her high standards.

Lara was gone when I got home. A note on the fridge said her mama Roberta was feeling poorly. Lara was over to her mother's, seeing to her little half-sisters. I called Lara at Roberta's and told her I'd got a sturgeon for Uncle Elmer. Lara could claim her wedding dress. I'd had such a long day I was going to nap before I cleaned it. I had a few hundred pounds of fish to attend to. It would put me out real late.

I drove out of Mountaindale just before midnight when the cops change shifts. Wasn't supposed to be driving, on account of my recent DUI. Got caught a week after I got out of jail. Two beers is all. My count was so close to the legal limit it was defensible, my attorney said. I went to court and took my lumps. I 'fessed up to the judge. She respected me for that. She let me off with ten days' time served and six months suspended.

No more screw ups, I'll be driving my bride to her honeymoon to the Empress Hotel up in Victoria, B. C. My aunt at Mountaindale Travel got me a deal on a three-day weekend with thirty-six months to pay. Takes me the rest of my life, I want Lara to have the fanciest wedding dress she can find and a glorious honeymoon.

Some nights shine like pale days along the Columbia Gorge. Oh Lordy but that night was bright. The moon shined like a Liberty quarter and the stars winked at me. I needed deep darkness, but what choice did I have? I had to finish the job. Once I hit the Gorge and took 14-West back toward White Salmon, I was feeling good. The traffic was a mile across the Columbia, way over on I-84, the Oregon side, the cops too. On my side, it was nothing but kids out prowling.

I pulled my old truck into a turnout high on the riverbank, set my cooler on the tailgate and found the deer trail that leads down to the spit where I'd tied up my fish. The sturgeon had swam off the shore, played out her line. She fought me as I hauled her in so I rolled her on her back. I had one hand on the lasso line and my knife ready in the other when I was flooded with light. A gravelly voice told me to hold it right there. That knife of mine went right ahead and sliced clean through the line. I can't say why. I couldn't breathe. All the air had been let out of me.

I stuck to my story. I'd caught the sturgeon and tied her up while I attended to Daddy who was feeling poorly. I'd come back to cut her loose. By some instinct I'd released the evidence against me. The sturgeon swam away, thank the Good Lord.

Galen Winthrop smirked, told me I was his main suspect the minute he noticed there was no bow line on our boat. I wouldn't be the first poacher who tied up a sturgeon and went back to harvest it later. He also said I was in violation on the DUI. I'd sit in jail while the sturgeon poaching was under investigation. All the way back to Mountaindale, Galen lectured. "Just because your family has been here forever, Donny Ray Carter, you figure the law does not apply to you."

"A hardship case," I said, wishing I had a beer. I was not drunk mind you. Had not been drunk all day. I couldn't blame alcohol. It was my rash and terrible need to be of service and to please my beloved. Preacher Winthrop's lips disappeared. He held up his hand and sawed his forefinger across his thumb.

"Do you know what this means, Donny Ray?"

"Can't say as I do, sir."

"I'm playing a sad song for you on the world's smallest violin. Now, a man might take a fish to feed a hungry family so long as it's a legal fish. A keeper sturgeon must be at least forty-two inches and not over sixty. A seven or eight foot sturgeon like you took is going to be a spawning female.

"Yes sir. Maybe that sturgeon was over size and maybe not. Who is to say when the evidence swam away?"

"The Department sets the size limits to preserve the big females for spawning."

"Yes sir." If Galen could convert a heathen, he might let me off.

"A six-foot female will be some twenty years old."

"That so, sir?"

"Took her ten years if not twelve just to mature."

"Yes sir."

"She's spawned but once every three years, five maybe."

"Is that so, sir?"

"You damn well know it, Donny Ray. There's a hundred fifty thousand keepers in the Columbia right now. There's no excuse for taking a big mature female."

"No sir, and I didn't."

"We'll see."

It seemed like the deputies at the Mountaindale jail yapped at me for years on end. I knew better than to open my mouth. When they finally gave me some change and told me I could make one phone call, I didn't bother with the law. I called Lara instead.

She was up watching some movie about a Greek wedding. Lara was going on about the wedding dress. Mama Roberta had a plan. Her artist friend could copy the dress. Her seamstress aunt could sew it; her friends from the Dead Heads could find crystal beads. Roberta herself would sew them pretties on.

"It's the nicest thing Mama ever did for me," Lara said, breathy in her voice.

Roberta's plan was inspired by pot charge number four, it seems. Number four meant jail is what the judge said last time. Unless her attorney can get her hearing postponed, Roberta won't make her daughter's wedding. But Lara's dead set against changing the wedding date. Said if she had to wait for Roberta to get off pot before she got married she might wind up an old maid.

I couldn't talk. My throat felt stuffed with wadding. My face blurred in the nickel plate of the pay phone. I needed a shave.

"Donny?" Lara said, "You there?"

I cleared my throat. "Lara, darling, I see you coming down the aisle to me as dazzling as a rainbow in a fog."

"Oh, Donny." Lara's voice went coy. "How you talk."

I couldn't bear to tell Lara I was back in jail. I'd jeopardized my wedding on account of a dress Lara no longer cared for. Put cash money on that dress this minute Lara'd say no. She's the dearest person on the planet. Lara would no more hurt Mama Roberta's feelings than she'd fly. I felt like I'd been embalmed. I took to my cot and slept like what I was—a dead man.

It was then I saw myself dressed in my bright orange jumpsuit. I had rubber slippers flapping on my feet. My toenails was claws. I needed a shave and stank like a sturgeon. I stood at the altar next to Lara. She dazzled in her satin, lace, and crystal beads. Came time for me to slip the wedding band on her finger next to the amethyst ring. I could not do it, no matter how I struggled.

Galen Winthrop was best man, smirking in his black beard. He'd cuffed my hands behind my back. He stood next to me, watching me struggle, stroking his forefinger down his thumb, playing a sad wedding song for me on the world's smallest violin.

MY THOUGHTS ON MILLIE MCCALL'S FULL MOON POKER NIGHT

by jd daniels, poet, novelist and editor for
Prairie Wolf Press Review

In Millie McCall's Full Moon Poker Night, Sara Williams, an author with a literature and journalism background, artfully drops clues by her choice of language, imagery and comparisons that an ancient story lurks not far below the surface of her tale.

This tightly woven novella is an intelligent, modern day Medusa story with multiple twists and character reversals. In Greek mythology, the rape of the beautiful Medusa by Poseidon, The Lord of the Sea, is witnessed by Athena, the Goddess of courage, wisdom and inspiration. The outraged jealous Athena who witnesses the rape takes her wrath out on Medusa, transforming her into an accursed monster with snakes for hair. Anyone gazing at Medusa will be turned into stone.

Millie McCall is described as a waif-like woman with a "snarl of sun-bleached brown hair." She arrives at an inn on Orcas Island for her poker game in a red flimsy negligee covered by a Harley Davidson leather jacket, to avoid outright indecency. In the eyes of Jim Halprin, the young narrator, Millie is 'a freaking mess.' Her hair hadn't met a comb in the last twenty-four hours and her brows needed mowing. She clumps about in Heavy Doc Marten boots. She smokes cigars. She has an involuntary tic and an attitude of weariness or grief. Like Jim, she rides a Harley. And like Medusa, her power enchants, but brings fear to the hearts of all men who know her; except her wealthy husband who, surrounded by young starlets, claims undying love for his wife. In Ted McCall we find snippets of two of the mythological characters: Athena—as he shackles his free spirited wife with medication and a padded room; and Poseidon, the man who raped Medusa, bringing her to her demise.

Jim sports a braid down his back, a Fu Manchu mustache and leathers that make the appropriate creaks. He arrives at the party as a stand-in for a local lodge owner, Ben Bridges, who has just been injured in a freakish accident. Ben is a 'wild-child' much admired by Jim's own powerful father and revered as a great man by the son. Ben warns Jim to flee the poker party when the last card slaps the table.

Unfortunately, Jim lingers on, enchanted by Millie's reckless charm and dangerous antics. Jim is an innocent and sensitive hero and he witnesses a magical transformation in Millie as she strides to a land bridge to a tiny atoll where she salutes the full moon at the end of the game. Millie's newly found energy renders her into a beautiful, well-kept woman, and here we find another role reversal on the myth. Ugliness to beauty. Not beauty to monster.

On a mad ride around the island chasing after Millie, Jim has an accident, is injured, hobbled, and realizes he has lost his summer job and quite possibly his college career. Thus, Millie has destroyed Jim's life as he knew it, or at least turned it into temporary stone. Jim suffers the curse of Medusa.

Williams provides us with a male hero who recognizes the child within himself and sees the child in Millie. He cannot bring himself to abandon her and soon becomes entangled in the network of spell-bound islanders who do their best to let Millie enjoy her dangerous antics while conspiring to keep her from harm. The injured Jim eventually finds himself back at the McCall mansion riding in the same wheelchair equipped with restraints meant to subdue Millie during the worst of her downer moments, a poignant irony.

Many current critics label Medusa a character thought to symbolize the rage of fettered women who desire freedom above all else. Through this dark but often humorous novella, Williams drives this message home as Millie's husband is being wooed by a Hollywood producer desperate to find funding for a feminist road picture, *Thelma and Louise*, being screened at a very hush hush business meeting at the McCall Mansion. Millie steals the show, her face filled with joy and relief as she makes her own bid for everlasting free.

Also by Sara Williams

The Don Juan Con

and two John Spyer Mysteries

The Serenoa Scandal

and

One Big Itch